OPENING
THE DOOR TO
CLOSE
THE DEAL

OPENING
THE DOOR TO
CLOSE
THE DEAL

**THE 7 MISTAKES THAT CAN
KILL NEW CLIENT ACQUISITION**

SCOTT THOMAS

CREATOR, SOCIAL DYNAMIC SELLING SYSTEM

Opening the Door to Close the Deal: The 7 Mistakes That Can Kill New Client Acquisition

BMD Publishing
All Rights Reserved

ISBN # 978-1093617009

BMDPublishing@MarketDominationLLC.com
MarketDominationLLC.com

BMD Publishing CEO: Seth Greene
Editorial Management: Bruce Corris
Technical Editor & Layout: Kristin Watt

Printed in the United States of America.

ACKNOWLEDGMENTS

From an early age, I had a goal-oriented drive for practically everything I did. It manifested in many ways and affected me and the people around me in different ways. As a student of human nature, the response and feedback that I received from others is what has taught me the most.

I want to start by thanking my brother and sisters from the very beginning for putting up with my "spirited' zest for life. I learned so much from our interactions. You have helped shape my success from an early age, while always keeping me grounded.

To my wonderful parents; you did an absolutely perfect job of guiding me while letting me explore "my way". As an excellent example of how to treat others, you are the deep roots of my belief that you should always put people first. I am very proud of the love and legacy that you instilled in all of your children. I love you both!

 A big thank you to my best friend and business partner Rylee Meek, for your boundless energy and drive to create the best experience for our clients and staff. I also want to acknowledge my numerous business mentors along the way who showed me good examples of TEAM. And all our employees behind the scenes and out on the road, who help create the culture that makes our clients so happy.

To Bruce Corris, for helping me get this message out into book form. I couldn't have done it without your expertise, efficiency and professionalism.

But mostly, I want to thank my beautiful wife Susan and daughter Hannah for their continued support. To Susan, the term "behind every good man is a great woman" has never been truer than with us. You are a great wife and wonderful mother. I love you so much! To Hannah, I am so proud of you, you have taught me more than you'll ever know. I admire your drive and resilience. You are a beautiful, creative, smart, strong young lady. I can't wait to see and experience the future with you both.

INTRODUCTION

A sales manager was addressing his underperforming sales team at the start of a new month:
"We're going to have a sales contest this month. The winners will get XYZ prize."

That's one type of sales coaching. Which can be effective in certain situations. But it's definitely not sustainable in the long run to an underperforming team.

And to have success, you need to have a sustainable process. Which means sales and marketing have to be a unified team, each understanding what the other does, and both working toward a common goal: acquiring clients.

That's what I've helped companies do for nearly 30 years. Clients ranging in size from small start-ups to Fortune 100 companies seeking seven-figure sales increases.

I take a different approach than most "sales coaches". Because I don't just look at the sales pitch, I look at the entire conversation that led to that pitch. A conversation that involves multiple people using multiple mediums. But with one unified message.

Because it's all too easy for that conversation to veer off course, or hit a brick wall, or for someone to do something that makes it virtually impossible to close that deal.

I've identified 7 common mistakes that can cause that to happen. They're common, but even experienced and successful marketing and salespeople aren't aware of them.

So let's get the conversation started, and get you started on opening more doors and closing more deals.

Scott Thomas
June 2019

TABLE OF CONTENTS

CHAPTER 1

WHO AM I?

Thank you for picking up this book. Hopefully it will be a while before you want to put it down.

So why are we here? I'm here to help you. But what kind of help are you looking for? Sales? Marketing? Both? While technically you would call this a sales coaching book, are you looking for a sales book? It's really much more than that. It's about working together, and literally being on the same page. It's about one person starting a conversation and another knowing how to finish it. It's about making sure they both know it's all one conversation. If you can get your message straight you're always going to get more sales.

If you're not sure where I'm going with that, hang in there. It will become clear to you. And once it does, once you say, "Now I get it", it will change the way you do things and change the results you get.

But before we get to that point, I'd like you to understand who I am and why I'm doing this. To do that, it will help to know how I got here. That being this point in my career and my life. It's been an interesting journey, filled with U-turns and an occasional dead end. So be prepared to say, "Huh. I didn't see that coming." Because I've said that a lot along the way.

Let's begin at the beginning. I was born in a very small town in Western New York, southeast of Buffalo. So you know what that means. Winter. But not too many of them, since we moved to Clearwater, Florida just before I turned five.

I was the third of four children, two girls and two boys. And if you've heard the stereotypes about a third child, they're all true in my case. Type-A personality, you can see (and hear) me coming a mile away.

It was what most people would call a normal childhood. Two parents, strong religious upbringing. We went to church every Sunday and Wednesday, my mom was the church secretary, and my dad was chairman of deacons. Most of my friends were from church, so that's who I spent most of my time with. Except Sundays. That was family day. When we got home from church I had to play with my brothers and sisters, and then we'd have a family dinner.

I always got along with my siblings, but in some cases we were polar opposites. My brother never got into fights or caused trouble, while I was always getting into something. If my parents ever needed to scold him, it would ruin his day. My parents could scream at me for 20 minutes, and I'd be thinking, "Okay, are you done? Cool, let's go!" On the other hand, my younger sister is more assertive, like me. She's a school teacher, and her students (and their parents) know not to mess with her.

My older sister is a bit older, so growing up, she was also many times our babysitter. And it was during that time that I began to understand the power of words. Like any kid, I was always trying to get away with things. But in my case, I was consciously thinking about what I would say and how I would say it. I remember practicing, "Okay, word it this way. No, word it this way. She's not going to like the first one." I knew how to say things to her, and to my parents, and my other siblings.

So even then, I was all about the message. At the time, the adults called it manipulation. But I kept thinking, "How do I get things to go my way when I think they aren't going to?"

Flashback to kindergarten. I had just gotten glasses. Remember, I was assertive. I wanted to play Dodge Ball. But they don't pick the kid with the glasses. So if I thought I wouldn't get picked for a game, I just went and started another game and got people interested in that one. Because I knew if it was my game, I'd get to play. So there's another thing I learned early on. Don't sit and wait for others to do it. You have to do it yourself.

Another thing I remember from my school days is sports. Specifically, team sports versus individual sports. I wasn't a big fan of team sports because even if you sat on the bench, if the team won you'd get the same credit as the guy who played every day. I never liked that payoff. So I became a wrestler in high school. I knew if I won, I'd get all the credit, and if I lost, I was the only one to blame. I felt I could succeed if I stayed focused.

Not that I was the best student. No straight A's for me. Lots of B's and C's and even the occasional D. I just knew I wasn't studious. I also had a short attention span. I was always thinking of the next thing. I'm still doing that. But high school taught me I probably wasn't college material, and while I had no clue what I wanted to do for a living, I knew I didn't want to work for someone else. I didn't want a boss. I wanted my own business.

Then came the shark.

I was taking Oceanography in the eleventh grade. We did a lot of dissecting in that class. For our final project, we had to dissect a little shark. The teacher told us since the final exam would involve us identifying a shark's organs, we should draw what we saw. My drawing was pretty lifelike. It looked more like a black and white photo than a drawing. My teacher said, "Wait a minute. You drew that?" I said yes. He asked me if he could have it. He said if I gave him the drawing he'd give me an A on the final and I wouldn't even have to take it. Needless to say, I gave it to him right away.

Until that day, I just assumed everyone could draw. That's what my dad did. He was a sign maker, and could draw and paint. But when I realized not everyone could do that, I also realized I could use art skills to my advantage. That could be my business. I thought, "There has to be a way people make money doing art." So I began looking into things. A friend's father was the marketing director of the company that owned Eckerd Drugs, and he told me they employed artists. I said, "I could make a living doing this?" He said I could actually make a lot of money. So I asked him how to start. He asked his artists, and they said I should go to art school. So about two weeks after I graduated high school, that's what I did. I learned all the basics, including three weeks of learning how to draw a line so there's no little bulb at the end when you pick the pen up.

One important thing I learned was while I was thinking about how to sell the mechanism of art, what people really wanted was someone who could convey a message better than they could. Basically, the difference between an artist and a marketing artist. Because you needed more than just, "this looks good," you needed something that told the story and gave people a reason to do something.

I learned that through headlines and graphics and the way you lay things out, I could easily get humans to respond in a different way by just changing what they see. I could prove it. I'd send two versions out and I could predict which would do better. And I got better and better at that.

So remember what I said about never working for someone else? I started working for other people. I worked for agencies, small companies, and one very big company, BIC, where I started in the art room and worked my way up to marketing director. I took those jobs because I still didn't understand how to start my own business from scratch. So I worked, and I learned things. And I knew I would learn how to go out on my own.

That's what happened at BIC. We used various companies as vendors. I became friendly with some of these business owners, who taught me the ropes. So when I left BIC, I opened my own agency. And I wanted BIC as a client. Think about that. I had to figure out a way to do that correctly so I wouldn't burn a bridge and they'd actually accept me as a vendor. This had to be very carefully communicated. Think about it, it's like trying to give your parents financial advice as they get older. You can be the #1 advisor in your area, but they changed your diaper. I was in the art room four years ago, now I wanted to be their vendor telling them what to do and who to sell to. Employee who leaves, makes more money on the outside, charges them a lot, and keeps a good relationship. But it worked really well, because I got their two biggest projects of the year along with a steady flow of small projects. I was off and running.

I began using what I had learned early in life about messaging. I would tell clients, "When we do lead generation a certain way, this is what you should tell your sales manager." They couldn't understand what a sales manager had to do with it. Their job was just to get leads. I'd say, "Yes, but if you get leads and they can't sell them, your job's not safe. Who gets fired first? Sales is revenue, marketing is an expense." I told customers that if they couldn't connect their lead generation to the same conversation of a salesperson to close it, the salespeople would tell the bosses the leads were lousy. And even if the marketing people said the salespeople were weak, they'd lose that battle.

It's not a gap between A and B, it's a brick wall between them. There might be one kind of voice in one conversation and a different voice in another one. You can't change your voice midstream. You have to understand the continuum from, "Hi, my name is," to, "Thanks for the order." The two components have to work together, and when one hands off the baton to the other, don't let go until they know it's firmly in the other one's hand.

I've actually always told people, "You should compensate sales and marketing people on each other's job." See how much each helps the other then. Because if the marketing director only got paid on sales that closed and the sales manager only got paid on number of leads, see how fast they'd fight for the other person's position.

It still comes back to what you say and how you say it. Say you're writing copy to start your conversation in direct mail. Picture the recipient checking their mail while standing over a garbage can. "Yep, yep, nope, yep, yep, nope, yep." You have half a second to get them to say, "Hold on, I want to read this." When they open, you can't let them down. You have to start your conversation the right way. Think about your marketing conversation, all the way through to your sale. Your message is often, "Sale! Urgent! All I care about is the dollars!" Then you try to tell them you just want to help as many people as you can, and that's when the conversation starts to fall apart. You changed the bait when you were pulling. You can't do that. The lure can't change.

Remember, I learned a lot about this early on, growing up one of four siblings with four different personalities, with parents whose personalities were different than all of us. I had to figure out how to get what I wanted by using words differently. Some of it was intentional, to disrupt and create a big scene, knowing that once they recovered, my parents would give me what I really wanted. As I said earlier, when you're a kid, adults call that manipulation. But it's really marketing. It's all about what your message is. What message do you want to convey to the right person to get them to do what you want them to do?

You need to be goal oriented and focused on a plan. Manipulation has a negative connotation, because it's as if you were tricked into doing something. But I could argue no one is ever tricked into doing something they really don't want to do. Or buy something they really don't want to buy. The salesperson might have told you why you should buy it, even why you should want it….but you did really want it in the first place.

Take my daughter, who's in high school. I've tried to teach her that when she talks to a teacher because she doesn't understand something, always think about their motivation. Why should they want to help? If a student says, "You were going so fast I couldn't write it all down," that's blaming them. But if instead that student says, "I think I got it right but can you check to make sure my notes are right before I go home and study this?" the teacher will be happy to help.

At some point in my life, I really got focused on this. Then once I got focused on it, I got better at it. And once I got better at it, I extended to showing other people how to do it and they got better, which proved it works. To my mind, there's the continuum of "I've heard about it," then "I know it," then "I'm convinced," then "I'm convicted." I'm well into convicted. I can prove it in every different direction. And I can teach you how to do it, so you can do it, too.

Once you get really clear about it and what your goals are, you also have to clearly understand your customer so you can speak to them the way they want to be spoken to, and understand the method you're using to speak to them. It's not just verbal. It can also be a text, an email, direct mail, even a billboard. So you need to understand your medium. You can use funky acronyms in texts and emails. You can't use jargon on a robocall. What can you do and what can't you do? Just keep coming back to that garbage can image. Is it going to pass the garbage can test?

There's a term I often use to describe myself. "Human Response Expert". Because frequently customers will say things like, "Hold on, I'm from New York and it's totally different here." No it isn't. Humans are humans. We may talk with a different accent depending on where we're from, but when it comes down to it, all humans will respond the same way. As long as you go to their instincts, and you go for natural responses.

A big part of all this is understanding where the conversation is, and where you are in the conversation. That leads to natural progression. Don't fight that, let it happen the way it should.

Picture a man taking a woman on a first date, and before they order dinner he says, "I just want to let you know, of course I'm going to pay for dinner, and we'll have some drinks, and then at some point I'm going to bring up the idea of you coming back to my house or me coming back to yours. So before you order, let's make sure we're both on the same page." How do you think that's going to turn out? He literally killed the natural progression.

Hopefully that actual conversation never happens, but things like that do happen all the time. It's like those special offers. "One day only!" Then it's extended for two more. And we know even if the offer ends Thursday and we call Friday, the offer is still going to be there. The coupons we always get in the mail for Bed Bath and Beyond have an expiration date, but we can always use them weeks, months, even years after they "expire".

At one point, I was the marketing director of a marketing company. Doesn't that sound like fun? I had to teach salespeople to think like a marketing person, and marketing people how to understand sales. Which forced me to simplify the other side's role. I had to take all sales & marketing jargon out. Bear in mind, when you get a room full of marketing people, they could all be talking Klingon and they'd understand each other. Once you start talking to anyone else, including salespeople, you've lost them. So I've had to break things back down, and honed it down to the point where I could say, "Okay, I get it." That's where the "Human Response Expert" title comes in. I understand how humans work. I know how to play human chess in every scenario, whether it's a social/social setting, a business/social setting, or a business/business setting. And while I remained the marketing director, I actually took over sales.

Sales is all about understanding the buyer. How they buy and how they think. And then honing your message to reach them in the most effective way. Which includes direct mail. Take financial advisors. Nearly every piece of mail they receive is serious. Serious documents, forms people need to sign, all in white #10 professional-looking envelopes. When I was trying to market to financial advisors as clients, I knew I needed to disrupt that. So I hired a cartoon artist to create a postcard. One side had a cartoon of a guy looking at his phone and a woman asking him what he was doing. He said, "Waiting for my phone to ring." Then on the other side was a different cartoon saying "Your phone won't ring on its own. You need help with your marketing." Everyone laughed at me and said, "You're sending financial advisors a cartoon?" I said, "Yes, because no one else will do that." We got a huge response. Six times the industry average.

One important distinction I like to point out is that there are really two versions of marketing. One is active, the other is passive. A billboard is passive. You put it up and hope people see it. Traditional media ads, on television and in newspapers, are also passive. Active marketing is when you're going to get them. You're mailing. You're reaching out. You're touching. Oftentimes, people think they can keep layering on passive methods and get bigger and bigger results. But if your marketing isn't a lever, when you push it forward do you get more? If you pull it back, do you get less? In direct mail, if you mail 10,000 pieces you get X. If you double it to 20,000, you'll get twice as much. If you cut back to 5,000, you'll get half as much. So when people realize that and start to see it work, they'll literally take all the money out of their budget for passive methods, move it over to active methods, and see their business explode.

But you have to understand how the lever works. That's a big part of what we teach our clients. If you get in your car and hit the gas pedal, it doesn't do any good unless you're in gear. You have to know what you're doing. You have to know your numbers, be clear about your product, and you really have to know your customer. When we get somebody's mind to shift, that's when they get it. It's almost like being in the military. You start with boot camp and it's uncomfortable, but once you get it, you really get it. And that's when you truly feel like you're driving your company. You're actively in control of your business.

People often tell me, "You're a marketing guy, why should I come to you for help with sales?" The reason is, marketing is just the beginning of a conversation that should be ending in a sales conversation. And at some point or another, it should become one continuous conversation. So a marketing guy should want to understand how his salespeople are selling the product or service, so he can start the conversation correctly. On the other hand, he might find out they're just not very good at selling it.

What I do is help marketing people start the conversation better, and salespeople end it the right way.

I get it, there are tons of people out there who say they can help you with sales. And they tell you to know your numbers and keep a funnel. Count your prospects, keep track of this and that, make more calls and get more referrals. Those are all great things, but that's like telling a kid in Little League, "You have to hit more. You have to get on base more." That doesn't help. You're telling him he needs more results, but you're not showing him how to do that. You're not showing him how to hold his hands, how to swing the bat, how to keep his eye on the ball. You have to give actual, tactical direction. That's what I do. Complete with telling you what to say next and why to say it. There's that conversation again.

There's a strategy to selling. And marketing leads to strategy. Here's an analogy. I took karate so I could learn how to slow down. So I could learn how to see things coming. Because if you go into a fight thinking you're going to out-work your opponent, it's possible you'll be able to do that, but you can out-work yourself too. You can tire yourself out. As boxers say, you can punch yourself out.

But if you can slow down and predict things better, you can make a more specific and more strategic move. So if you clearly understand how a full conversation works, then when somebody starts a sentence or asks you a question, you can predict where they're going. And if you don't like where it's going, you can change the direction. You're in control of the conversation. Whether you're in sales or marketing, you should be trained at your job, and trained on your product and your customer.

If you understand your customer, you understand how to talk to them, you understand when to talk to them, beginning to end, marketing all the way through sales, then when you lay out your plan, you know that you're pushing the right lever and when you do, now that lever is moving something.

There are sales coaches and marketing coaches, but in reality, they're just different versions of people all saying the same thing. They tell you what to say on a call, and how to write copy for your letter. But does anybody ever say the copy in your letter is dictating what you should be saying on your call? Does anyone ever say this is what got their attention and this is how you should be finishing the conversation? Unfortunately, what happens a lot of times is that brick wall goes up between sales and marketing. Marketing sends out lead generation pieces and sales gets a bunch of leads, but then the salespeople don't continue the conversation that was started. They start from scratch. And then they each blame the other for the lack of conversions. But neither side realizes that the prospect is halfway through a conversation, and if that conversation didn't flow properly, they get lost.

Picture yourself watching the movie, *Superman*. The movie starts and there's this superhero wanting to save the world, but feeling like an outsider. Now imagine you don't know the background. You don't know he came from another planet, and how he survived its destruction. You'd be really confused with the movie. At a minimum, you wouldn't connect with the character.

The same holds true for the marketing and sales conversation. If it doesn't flow properly, the prospect is confused or disconnected. The prospect doesn't become a buyer. They're not interested. And you did that to them. Which brings me back to what I said about marketing people spending time with sales and sales feedback, and salespeople reading every marketing piece that goes out. It's all one conversation.

All of which brings me back to this book, and why we're here. Chances are, you're here for one of three reasons. You may be part of a sales team that's struggling with closing deals, and struggling with your marketing people. You may be a marketing person who's struggling with your sales team. Or you may be a business owner who keeps thinking if you just outwork other people you'll do great. That's the normal entrepreneurial scenario. But all that leads to is working harder and working longer and running out of hours and burning yourself out.

Whatever role you're in, this book will help you understand the continuum. It will help you work better with the others, and get better results.

On the other hand, if you're reading this book because you're a salesperson and your manager told you to read a book so you could learn something from it, stop right now. Put this down and move on. You have to want to be here. Sales and marketing can be learned but you have to have an internal motivation.

I wrote this book with a certain type of person in mind. It has nothing to do with where you are in your career or how much money you make. It has everything to do with your mindset. It's how you look at things, and how much you want it.

It's also about whether you get it. Whether you understand just how important it is to really interact with others. As I said earlier, we're all humans. Whether you're from Portland, Maine or Portland, Oregon. The accents are different, the humans are the same. Think about that one kid in high school. He wasn't the best looking, he wasn't the best jock, he wasn't the coolest, but he always had attention. Even as a high school student, he knew how humans work. Some people just naturally have that.

But don't worry if it doesn't come to you naturally. As long as you understand the importance of it, you can learn the rest.

Which is why we're here. So let's get started.

CHAPTER 2

WHO ARE YOU?

Okay, now that you know more than you probably wanted to know about me, let me share a little of what I know about you. Because if you're the type of person who should be reading this book, I've worked with many people just like you. And yes, I feel your pain.

Chances are, you're one of three types of people. You're in sales, and you're dependent on revenue for your success, or even your job. Or you're a marketing person whose success or job also depends on revenue, or the acquisition of new clients. Or you own the company, and you have to wear one or both of those hats in order to grow your business, or maybe just to survive.

But no matter what your role, if revenue or new client acquisition matters to you, picking up this book was a good call.

For a lot of salespeople, the struggle is dealing with that endless cycle. Their world starts on the first of the month, and no matter how successful they are, the first of the next month rolls around and they're back at zero, and they have to start all over again.

If you're living in that constant churn, chances are you're facing these challenges. How do you get in front of more people, how can you close the deal with more of the people you're in front of, and how can you sell more to the people who buy?

If you're in marketing, it's a similar scenario but slightly different, because chances are you're measured on things like number of leads or client acquisition cost. In other words, being efficient at your job. So you have two things: how to get more leads, and how to keep the costs down. Or better yet, how to keep the cost where it should be. Because lower doesn't necessarily mean better. High volume at a low price would probably flood your salespeople and frustrate them. You want the best quality leads for the lowest amount, even if it's not all that low.

As for the entrepreneur, you're trying to do all these things. And chances are you don't know how to do most of them, or any of them for that matter. Most business owners don't know how to close a sale, or get more leads, or be more efficient. They just know they love what they do, and they're probably honest and very passionate about their craft. So you understand your business, but you may not know how to sell or market it at the highest level of efficiency.

Compounding the issue is the fact that salespeople and marketing people often compete with each other. This one lowers the price and gets more volume, and that one says "Sure, we have more leads, but they suck." And the owner has to juggle all of this.

Whatever role you're in, you're probably also dealing with how your business looks at sales and marketing. Or sales vs. marketing. Too often, companies look at marketing as an expense and sales as a revenue source. Every day, someone starts a business and says, "I don't need marketing, I can build this by word of mouth." Yeah, right. Whether you're a local pizza shop or a nationwide corporation, you have to do some level of marketing. And somewhere in that marketing, there's a customer you're communicating with, and how you communicate with that customer matters.

You may also be challenged by your sales cycle. That's a common issue for both sales and marketing people. Some salespeople only want volume and churn, and don't care about building relationships. Others can only sell by nurturing their clients, taking plenty of time and having plenty of meetings and building long relationships. That's another area where sales and marketing have to be on the same page, with the same message.

Here's a very important question. Do you know your client acquisition cost? Don't feel bad if the answer is no. Many people don't. And whatever your business, you have to know that number, so whenever you have to decide about a marketing method, you'll know whether it's worth the cost. In this case, the word expensive is a relative term. The actual dollar amount isn't as important as the relativity. If you sell something for $30,000, you may be willing to pay $5,000 for a lead. If you own that pizza shop, $50 a lead is too steep. You can talk to an online retailer who knows he can get leads for $1.12 each, and even if you can get him great leads for $1.25, he'll tell you it's not worth it. In some cases, $10,000 is cheap, and in other cases, $1.50 is pricey.

I hope this book will get you thinking about that. I also hope it will help open your eyes. Because if you haven't tossed me aside by now, you're willing to try new things because deep down, you know that's what it's going to take to get your business to the level you want.

Now that doesn't mean you aren't part of what I call the "D and D" crowd. That's *Doubters and Disqualifiers*. Doubters begin with the belief, "I don't think I could do this," or "It's too expensive," or my personal favorite, "There's no way this will work." But after they clean out their head trash and get rid of any barriers or walls they set up, and reach the point where they can say, "Okay, let me really look into it and examine it," the "aha" moment on the other side can be life altering.

The disqualifiers, on the other hand, have an understanding of different marketing methods, but they've seen other people do things that didn't work, so they go in with the mindset of, "I've seen this before and it didn't work then, why would it work for me?" The answer, of course, is because they either saw something different, or saw someone do it badly. And they tend to give that person credibility. "He's a smart businessman, I know he would have done it right." But you really have no way of knowing that. So if they get to the point of, "Well, this might make sense for me," they often find something that not only works for them, but works exceedingly well.

It also comes down to the teaching you get. For example, you may want to teach your son how to play basketball. But you may not be very good at it. So unless he has some Kobe Bryant skills you don't know anything about, his best-case scenario is he's only going to be as good as you are. Misjudging any marketing method because you've seen somebody else fail at it doesn't make sense.

I should tell you, I haven't just learned about you, I've also learned FROM you. There's an old saying that the best way to learn is to teach. (It's a very old saying. In fact, it's based on a Latin principle from thousands of years ago.) But it still holds true. You can practice and practice and practice, but when you can explain it to somebody else so they get it, that's when you will truly get it.

Because when you teach someone, you not only have to tell them what to do, you also have to explain why you do it, how to do it, what not to do and why not, and so much more. My "Aha" moment came when I realized I could duplicate this. Now I know I can take somebody who knows nothing about it, transfer everything I know to them, and they can go out and succeed on their own.

If you're who I think you are, that's what you're looking for, and that's why you're here.

CHAPTER 3

MANIPULATION VS. MARKETING

In my first chapter, when I was talking about my childhood, I talked about knowing what to say to my parents and siblings, and how to say it, to get the best results for myself. I pointed out how that was perceived as me knowing how to manipulate them, which is a negative connotation, but that in reality, it was my first learning experience with marketing.

Now, decades later, I'm still dealing with the whole idea of manipulation vs. marketing.

There are different ways to look at that, depending on who you are and what you do. If you're trying to become more successful in sales, you should be looking at the words you're using and how you're using them. But from the customer's perspective, if the salesman just left and you feel kind of icky because of the way he talked to you, you would definitely feel like you've been manipulated. So whether it's the words themselves or the tone, we really need to think about how they're perceived by those on the receiving end.

Look up manipulation in the dictionary. One of the definitions is, "to control or play upon by artful, unfair, or insidious means especially to one's own advantage." Ouch! Talk about a negative connotation.

When someone is described as manipulative, it's usually because they're perceived as always trying to get their way. Well, in sales, you ARE always trying to get your way. You're always trying to close the deal. If you're in business and trying to get a customer, you're trying to get your way. But that doesn't have to be a bad thing. If you're an ethical person with a good product or service, it should be a win-win situation. When there's a real value, and you can get the customer to understand that value, and you close the deal that way, you both win.

It all starts with having a plan. If I want to meet with someone and talk to them, and I have a goal for that conversation, I need a plan. I start with asking myself, "What's in it for them? What do they really need, and how do I deliver the message so they understand that what I'm offering is what they need, and there's a value for them?" If you don't know the answers to those questions already, then you need to plan your questions accordingly, then LISTEN.

I don't call that manipulation, I call that highlighting the points that matter to them. There are plenty of parents who say their children are trying to manipulate them. I don't think any parent would call their child's actions marketing. But every day, kids go through this process: "I want my mom to do something for me. If I ask it in this way, and she sees there's something in it for her, then she'll probably do it." Guess what? That kid is doing marketing.

At the end of the day, if your prospect thinks you manipulated them, you did it wrong. If you did it poorly, or didn't go through the natural progression and skipped some steps, you did it wrong. If your customer has buyer's regret, you did it wrong.

The most common excuse when someone has buyer's regret is, "I really didn't want this product. They talked me into it." But in reality, you're not going to talk someone into doing something they really didn't want to do.

If I'm trying to sell you a parachute and you have no intention of ever going skydiving, no matter how hard I try to manipulate you (and in this case it's the negative connotation of manipulate), there's no way I can trick you into buying. You're going to say, "I don't need this, I don't want this, I'll never need or want this."

When that car salesman is at the end of the month and trying to get his bonus, he's going to offer a better deal than he did on the fourth of the month. But no matter how good the deal is, if you need a pickup truck for your business, he's not going to talk you into a four-door sedan. On the other hand, if you go in wanting an SUV because you need the size and you want to carry many passengers, he can steer you (sorry, couldn't resist) to a sedan, and if it makes sense and is a better deal, you just might go that route. He may get you to say, "Well, it's not what I came in for, but it will do a lot of the things that I need, and it's really a good deal."

It's much easier to close the gap between "I want it and I have the money for it," to "This is a good deal. I want it today," than it is to close the deal when the customer begins with, "I know I want this, but I don't necessarily have the money for it right now. I could get it, but not today." That's where a good salesman helps them go ahead and make the decision now.

Many people believe most sales are an emotional purchase. And they are. "Is now the right time? Am I making a good decision? Will I regret this later?" The key question for you to be aware of is the middle question. Your job is getting them to believe they're making a good decision and making it for the right reasons. If you do it wrong, and they forget the benefit or the feature of the product, and all they remember is that icky feeling of you pushing and pushing until they finally just got rid of you. That's where manipulation comes in.

In sales, the opposite of "I like it and want it" isn't "I hate it, I don't want it." It's indifference. Complete indifference. "It's not for me. I don't care about it." This happens a lot in the restaurant industry. I've heard people say, literally, "I think I'm going to open a restaurant because everyone has to eat." Yes they do, but they don't have to eat at your place. For you to survive, enough people have to know about your restaurant, want to eat there...and then, like it enough to come back.

That's why understanding the customer is everything. Because you can't even come up with a plan of how to talk to them if you don't start by saying, "I understand them." If you don't understand them, you have almost no shot. And to understand them, you have to listen to them. How do you prove to somebody else that you're a great listener? You get them talking, and then listen to them. There's no trick to that.

In marketing, we look at people as suspects, before they become prospects. Once they show a slight level of interest, they're a prospect. And once they become a prospect, knowing their level of interest determines the next step in the conversation. If you're 80 percent, we can just tell you how to place the order. If you're five percent, we have some talking to do. And we want to get you talking so we can listen. And we can plan.

Back to that car salesperson. He needs to pull the right strings. If you came in looking for an SUV and he didn't ask any questions, or listen to your answers, he could miss the mark. If you need an SUV to tow a boat, talking about the seating capacity and how a sedan could hold just as many, would fail miserably. He wants to steer the conversation toward solutions to your specific concerns and not merely list features and benefits.

Knowing the customer's needs and interests lets you push the right buttons to motivate them. If you're selling solar panels, and the customer is big on saving the planet, you're not going to lead with how much they're going to save on their electric bill. You're going to lead with how this is going to preserve natural resources and leave the planet in better shape for their grandchildren. But if they're all about just saving money, the only green you should be referencing is the dollar bills they're going to be pocketing each month.

Is that manipulating? Yes. Is that a bad thing? Nope. We are only manipulating the emphasis on the topics and the flow of the conversation, not the actual facts. That would just be called Lying!

So go ahead and manipulate. The right way. Because after all, it's just marketing.

CHAPTER 4

SALES VS. MARKETING

I want to do a little deeper dive into the issue of sales vs. marketing, as opposed to sales WITH marketing. In many companies and organizations, you have sales on one side and marketing on the other, and instead of working together, they're butting heads.

One reason for that is money. For example, in a company that's large enough to have a sales department with a sales manager and a marketing department with a marketing manager, the way they're measured puts them at odds. Many companies break up their budget so that marketing is an expense and sales is a revenue. So a dollar over here is worth it because you're going to get it back, and a dollar over there is expensive, because you don't know what's going to happen.

There's an old saying, "I'm wasting half of my marketing budget, but I don't know what half so I have to keep spending it." A lot of companies will look at their budget and see how much they're spending, and how much sales they're getting, and think if they cut the spending in half they'll lose half their sales, or if they double it, their sales will double. Which isn't the case. Remember, salespeople are measured on sales and marketing people are measured on leads or activity. They might say, "Look how active we've been this year, we've been to 20 trade shows." But what if half of them were a complete waste? The fact is, big cuts or increases in the wrong type of spending could have a very minor effect, while a small increase in certain areas could have a major impact.

A marketing department might say, "We spent this much money and got this many leads," and it might be a big number, but there may not be any value to those "leads". I've actually heard our customers say, "Oh, we have thousands of leads," but when I ask them where they came from, it turns out they simply bought a list. Those aren't leads, they're names on a list. I like to say, those aren't prospects, they're suspects. To a salesperson, a name on a list is nothing, and it should be. To a marketing person, when you have a name on a list, you have to get them to act or do something. Once they do, you likely changed them from a suspect to a prospect, so now you should be able to count that as a lead.

But I'll argue both sides, and say if anyone shows any more than zero percent interest, give them to the salespeople and let them do their job. Don't tell me leads are weak or bad or good. If they showed any kind of interest, and they fit any kind of criteria, you should be able to take it all the way. That's how I look at marriage. It isn't 50-50, it's 100-zero. And it should be. My relationship with my wife is 100 percent on me, and hers with me is 100 percent on her. If we do 50-50, we'll just blame the other person when something goes wrong. Marketing and sales should be the same way. Marketing should be working to get the highest level of interest they can, and sales should be willing to take someone from very little.

As a salesperson, you should never say leads are weak. Whether there's a 25 percent interest level, or 10 percent, or just one percent, you should want and be able to pull them the rest of the way. So as a marketing person, your job is to get them from nothing to something. Once there's something, then sales can go from there.

You'll hear me say this throughout this book. Always follow the primary rule: You have to begin with the end in mind. If you don't, it would be like going on a trip to a destination with no map and no idea how to get there. That doesn't mean you can't say, "I just want to travel the country, and I don't care where I go and when I get there." That's a great way to travel. But it's a terrible way to do sales.

It makes no sense for a business to say, "We don't care where we end up." You always care where you end up. You always have to begin with the end in mind. So look at how you judge through the sales cycle. What's the responsibility of the marketing department to get leads and how far do they need to get? If you make them go any more than halfway, you're probably setting yourself up to fail. Because you're saying, "I want the customer to show up with their wallet open, with money out, ready to buy...and then we'll turn it over to sales." You don't need sales then, you just need an order form.

I say the responsibility of marketing is to generate interest or awareness or any of that small first part, and sales takes the rest from there. So if you measure marketing just on number of leads, then sometimes you'll end up with just volume and tonnage for the sake of volume and tonnage. And be careful how you gauge interest. Sometimes people think because someone opened an email, they're interested. But it could just be they were swiping through, and yours is the one they picked when they started deleting. I think one of the biggest mistakes companies make is measuring number of leads and number of sales separately. That's what leads the two areas to butt heads. One may say the leads are weak, and the other may say the salespeople can't sell.

Because I've managed both sales and marketing, some say I have a unique perspective. I say I have a unifying perspective. Always thinking to begin with the end in mind. If it's a marketing scenario, I'll go to the end of a sale and think, "This person just said yes. What got them there?" Then back up from there. I'll do the same with sales. I might point out to them that if someone has zero interest in what we do or what we sell, it's impossible to get them to respond to our marketing materials. But if there's some interest, even the slightest amount, then it's up to us to show its value or benefit. Something has to attract them. Even a corn dog.

It's like fishing with a corn dog. This is one of my favorite analogies. There's no place in nature where fish eat corn dog. Period. But you can catch a fish with corn dog because it can generate interest, and it's something they would try or eat. There are fish that will try it. So you can use it to catch a fish. But you wouldn't use it to nourish that fish for life. So attracting a suspect to become a prospect is one thing. Making them a happy customer going forward is something else entirely. They're two different things, and you have to be okay with them being different.

In this case we are talking about marketing copy or offers. Saying too much too early can also sometimes have an adverse effect. Yes, corn dog can get their attention. Maybe your product is Grade-A beef, and your sales reps know all of the details of why it is Grade-A. Marketing comes along and sends out a piece that just indicates a singular value, and sales calls it weak… or corn dog. This is where the disconnect from attracting and selling begins. Sometime just getting suspects to think about the possibility of your product/solution is enough to get them started. Too much detail, or overselling, early in the relationship process can result in less attraction.

I always tell salespeople to read the lead generation piece that attracted your lead, so you can continue the conversation. That's where we've done a bad job in many if not most industries. The marketing director writes the letter to get the leads, and then either they don't share it, or they share it but don't tell the salespeople how to bridge that gap. Many times, marketing people are better writers and better story tellers than salespeople, although really good salespeople are really good story tellers.

So if I'm sitting with a salesperson, I'm saying, "Listen, this is where they were going. It's impossible for those prospects to have zero interest. So let's use that bridge that we talked about." But when I'm with marketing people, I'm saying, "Now when we write the lead, write the follow-up talking points. Write what the salesperson should say to somebody who responds to this lead."

Let's say the marketing showed you the risks or the dangers. The salesperson should show you how to get rid of those risks. The bridge could be, "Here are the benefits of why you should never do this on your own, and you should always hire a professional. Here's the difference between doing it yourself and you hiring a professional." Now they have the follow-up, not just the leads. Help build a bridge. And always understand how far to come across your side of the bridge.

When both sides can bridge the conversation, it becomes more effective. I'll tell marketing people, "Do more than just your job." And then I'll tell salespeople, "Do more and understand more than just your job." If they do that, they'll grow naturally into each other. No more thinking they just get paid to get closes or they just get paid to get leads. They'll actually talk to each other, and have a more effective conversation from beginning to end.

One of the things that helps build that wall between sales and marketing is the sales manager or marketing manager's acceptance of excuses. If a salesperson says, "My numbers are low because leads are weak," that's them blaming the other side. If the marketing people say, "Those guys can't close," same thing. It becomes this us versus them. But any good, strong sales or marketing manager will say, "No matter what happens, I could have done it better. I could have used better words. There's something I could have and should have done."

You need to lower that brick wall. Because it's not a level bridge, it's a bridge that goes up high over a high wall, and that makes it harder for each side to climb the bridge and get to the other side. And the wall is only as high as the sales manager and marketing manager will allow. It's up to them to lower the wall to make it easier to build a bridge, or make sure there's no wall there at all.

Maybe the sales manager can record the calls, and go through the words they use, and help them come up with more effective ones. Maybe the marketing people can give the salespeople copies of the emails, and copies of the talking points, and let them know that if someone responded to this email, this is likely what they're looking to hear. This should be a continuous, never-ending process.

It's the salesperson's responsibility to know what got their attention so you can pick up that conversation at the right place. It's the marketing person's job to share the information or any amount of help in that conversation. The marketing person needs to know when to use that corn dog and when to use steak. The salesperson needs to know what's on the menu.

It becomes sales with marketing instead of sales vs. marketing, when everyone begins with the end in mind. If you say, "I want to get here", and realize there may be five or six ways to get there, you can change the open. Let's say your product has five good benefits. Not features, solid benefits. Now you can start one piece of communication with this benefit and bring them through the rest of the conversation, and then sell it to them. You could start five separate conversations and bring each of them to the right conclusion.

You may be ending with the same product, but it's a different feature of that product. So you're taking different steps to get there. But every step is unified from the step before. If it's solar panels, one end result can be the savings on their electric bill. Another can be preserving the planet. Another can be their legacy, leaving their kids a home with no mortgage and no electric bill. As long as you always begin with the end in mind, there is a continuum of this conversation from the first introduction or the first piece of mail or the first email or however it started, all the way through to closing the deal.

It follows a straight path. However the conversation begins, must be the path to how it needs to end. But if that conversation begins one way, and as the conversation crosses the bridge, and suddenly the person carrying that conversation across the bridge says something different, now they've arrived at a whole different landing point. The conversation is going to pick up totally differently than the way it began, and you're probably not going to close the deal. If someone responded to your marketing trigger piece about saving the planet, but the salesman starts talking about lowering your electric bill, this creates confusion and a disconnect.

Always follow the primary rule: You must begin with the end in mind. If you know where you're going, you can get there. If you don't have a specific path in place for your prospect, you're just throwing things against the wall and hoping one sticks. And trial and error is going to fail more times than it will succeed.

CHAPTER 5

CASE STUDY:
SHOW ME THE MONEY

More and more companies are creating the position of Chief Revenue Officer. And they're smart to do so. It's someone who can manage sales, marketing, and more. And you know if they can do that, they understand client acquisition and how to keep the marketing-sales conversation on point.

Greg Duss has done that for some of the biggest names in the business world, including Coca-Cola, Walmart, and Whole Foods, and has held executive positions at giants such as Dell and AT&T.

I've worked with Greg many times and in many ways over the years. The best thing I can say about him is, "He gets it."

Scott: For those readers who have never come across a Chief Revenue Officer, why don't you talk about what you do, and where you're doing it now.

Greg: I was hired by GSP in November, 2018. The company is a leading provider of retail services. My mission is to transform brick and mortar retail into environments people would want to come and seek, instead of the digital counterparts on the web.

Scott: You've had a lot of success over the years.

Greg: Thank you for the plug. I've actually driven over $2.5 billion in incremental revenue for the Fortune 500 firms I've worked with. That's incremental, so it didn't happen overnight, but it's been a pretty good run.

Scott: Pretty good is an understatement. We've worked together in various ways since 2008. A lot of it has been focused on something which this book dives deeply into, which is the continuum of the marketing-sales conversation. We've had to fix a lot of those conversations and a lot of the processes at those companies. Talk a little about the conversation, and the roadblocks that can come up between its starting point and the closing of the deal.

Greg: One important thing I've seen in working with you is how well you listen, not just to the verbal conversation but also the body language and presentation tone and all those elements combined, and then create messaging in a very direct manner to engage someone and build on that relationship.

There are a lot of opportunities for roadblocks. But the best way to avoid them is to understand it's a single thread that stretches across all those communication elements. What you've been so impactful in doing for the businesses where we've worked together, is creating that thread so the messaging, the engagement, and the interaction are all relevant and unified, from inception to the closing of the deal and even post-deal, because the relationship doesn't end when the customer agrees to buy.

Scott: You mentioned the various communication elements. The very first of the 7 mistakes laid out in the book is not understanding the medium, and not using the same message across all mediums. Between the marketing component and the sales component and all the different mediums, it's so easy to veer totally off course.

Greg: Which is why it's so important to keep your message unified. People appreciate that steadfast messaging. They respect it, and buy into it, because they're buying into you as the individual, they're buying into the service you provide, and they're buying into your reputation. If someone is bouncing all over the place, they're going to be perceived as having, for lack of a better term, ADD when it comes to relationship management, which won't allow them to build the types of organizations and revenues you and I have been able to build.

Scott: Over the years, you've helped some huge companies. But even the best companies stumble along the way.

Coca-Cola is a good example. We all remember how New Coke turned out. Talk about mistakes you've seen, and how you've helped companies get back on track.

Greg: There are many examples. But they all have a common theme. As you preach constantly, the one thing that always rings true is you have to know who your audience is. You have to know that if you're selling something to an individual, it's something that individual is going to embrace, and it's going to be part of what they do or have done. When someone takes a shotgun approach, the methodology doesn't connect because the message isn't focused. When it is focused, you're reinforcing the value at every step of the way.

Scott: I'm glad you brought up knowing the audience. This book deals with that a lot, particularly knowing the "why". Why are they interested in what you have to offer? Not what you're offering, or how you do it. Why does it matter to them?

Greg: Understanding the why is of ultimate importance because it defines how the person's going to be able to reuse the product or service you have in future experiences along the way. I go back to our promotional products experience, where we were defining the why from a business perspective, and providing our end users with programs that allowed them to be able to take the product and service that we had, and use it to drive loyalty. Use it to drive influence, and promotions on additional revenue opportunities. It took that share of wallet perspective and really started to embed that and expand it over all product segments.

It was the Amazon approach, where you start looking and not just selling books. We were selling promotional products that expanded to all nine or 10 categories of promotional products that allowed us to be able to grow the organization exponentially because of our process.

The messaging and the service that we delivered allowed them to have immediate success with their business that drove the loyalty, that continued to drive the reoccurring revenue where people would come in and continually experience from that point forward.

Scott: Let's talk a little about sales and marketing, or more likely sales versus marketing, because in this continuum of the conversation, marketing opens the door and sales closes the deal. When they have that unified approach, and each understands not just what they're doing, but what the other is doing, that's when it is successful. But when they are each going in different directions, that's when the conversation hits a brick wall. You've overseen both sales and marketing. Talk a little bit about that unified approach.

Greg:　You bring up an excellent example of something I learned back in 1996 with AT&T. If you're going to own the process, you need to own both sides of the process. Both sales and marketing need to buy in to the fact that they're in conjunction, not counterparts to each other. They're two parts of the choir. They have different attributes to make them successful in what they do, but together it's a production, not a solo. It is very important to own both of those categories from a business owner perspective, so you're able to create and hold people accountable for that environment.

Strategy and sales and marketing are all very important in creating that unified message, that unified approach, and that singular view to the client. As you've said, it's so critical that from the very first introduction to the end result, all elements are constant and in concert together.

Recently here at GSP, we had a problem where marketing would create a lot of activity, but that activity didn't turn into revenue. The business development organization operated in its own silo, and was focused on its relationships with the existing infrastructure or network that it would have. What I have been able to do here is bring both together, so now we're developing a single script of music for everybody to speak from and sing from, and it allows them to align better together. Marketing now provides tools and resources to sales that sales has helped influence and build and develop, so when they're speaking to clients they're all speaking in the same tone, the same vernacular, the same interaction that was intended from a marketing perspective and executed from the sales angle.

TAKEAWAYS FROM THIS CHAPTER

- An important aspect to the marketing-sales conversation is "listening", not just to the verbal aspect but also the body language and tone.
- There are many opportunities for roadblocks, but the best way to avoid them is to understand there's a single thread that stretches across all communication elements.

Working with Greg to help him turn companies around has often focused on messaging. You have to know who your audience is, and how to sell your product or service in a way they're going to embrace. Avoid the shotgun approach and keep your message focused, which reinforces your value every step of the way. This stresses understanding the "why", and making sure that both sales and marketing need to buy in to the fact that they're in conjunction, not counterparts to each other.

CHAPTER 6

MISTAKE 1:
NOT UNDERSTANDING THE MEDIUM AND THE DELIVERY METHOD

This chapter isn't about the pluses and minuses of the different mediums we use in the marketing-sales conversation, although we will get into that a little. This is really about the big picture. It's looking at the overall conversation, the continuum from "Hi, my name is," all the way to "Thank you for the sale."

The medium matters. How the message is being delivered matters. So let's start with a 30,000 foot view of why these two things are so important.

Let's start by separating the message from the delivery method and the medium. Whatever your message is, those are just the words. How that message gets to people and how they receive it and interact with it, is all very different for the different mediums. It happens one way in direct mail, another way in email, a third on social media, a fourth on outdoor, a fifth on radio, a sixth on TV, and the list goes on. They're all different, so the same headline may not be as effective on one as it is on another, because of the way the person is interacting with that medium. It isn't necessarily the words you used, it's how you got the words to them.

So should you use the same message across all forms of medium? The short answer is, it depends. Which is why understanding the medium is so important. There are times you want them all to match, and there are times it won't work if they all match.

Here's an example. If all you're trying to achieve is brand recognition, then you want to be extremely consistent and you want to put it everywhere. If you want everyone to know, "We're under new management", or "Check out our new logo or slogan," and you want to get everyone used to seeing it for branding purposes, then you absolutely should keep it consistent.

But if your goal is to attract new clients, increase sales, have a special, or some other call to action, then the words you use on a banner ad on a website, versus a direct mail piece, versus a TV commercial, will probably be pretty different. They all may end with the same call to action or goal, but the way you deliver that message might be very different.

That's why understanding the medium will also help you understand how to get your message absorbed into the person who's actually seeing it. Because in order to do that, you need to understand HOW they're actually seeing it.

The conversation, from marketing opening the door to sales closing the deal, will in all likelihood travel across multiple mediums.

I always like to say your relationship with your prospective customer starts with your first trigger piece. Whether that's a piece of direct mail, an email, something on social media, a banner ad, a billboard, a radio or TV commercial, whenever someone sees it for the first time is the actual beginning of your relationship.

However you want to carry the conversation across different mediums, you can't be changing all the time because that confuses people. Maybe the first thing they saw piqued their interest, but then they saw another ad with a conflicting message. Now they're confused and thinking, "Maybe it's not the same place. That's weird, two different companies with the same name." Or sometimes you tried the same message across different mediums, and that's confusing people.

There are reasons to not do that. Because of the medium itself, not because it's not what you want to say. It's how people act when they're interacting with a medium. When you're reading mail you act a certain way. When you open email you act differently. When you listen to the radio and an ad comes on, that's another way to act.

When you're trying to begin the relationship, trying to open the door and generate the leads, you may actually use multiple mediums targeting the same people. That allows you to find out how those people respond. Some respond well to mail but would never open an email, while others respond to email but not social media, and so on. Seeing how people respond will help you determine the benefits of each medium in that particular usage. That doesn't mean you can determine the overall pluses and minuses of each medium, you can only determine them in this particular case with this particular audience. But that's still valuable information.

And it reinforces the point that the biggest minus is usually the belief that one message fits all. Take email. Is your campaign B2B or B2C? If it's B2B, chances are your recipient is in business mode. Sitting at their desk, going through their daily barrage of email from co-workers and colleagues and clients, knowing many of those emails will require them to take some type of action. If it's B2C, your recipient is more likely to be going through their email on their phone, knowing they're going to be deleting much of what they receive without opening them, unless they recognize the sender's name or are intrigued by the subject.

If you understand how people receive their email, both personally and for business, you can change your message accordingly. If they're working, talk to them like they're working. If it's personal and you want to try to catch their attention, that's a different message. It requires you to not only understand the medium, but also the audience.

It's the same for social media. A business social media site such as LinkedIn, or a business' Facebook page, interacts with people very different than consumer-to-consumer or friend-to-friend or family-to-family on Facebook. As you're marketing to them, you have to understand how the person is going to receive your message. Each will be different.

If you're using radio or TV ads, it's pretty clear how people are receiving them. Most people are either listening to the radio in their car, or it's in the background in their office. They're not going to be able to respond to a call to action that sends them to a website. That's why so many radio ads use a phone number that's easy to remember, like 1-800-Call Now. Someone who's driving isn't going to easily write down a phone number. But if the ad captures their interest and the number is easy to remember, it can be successful. Someone who's watching television could be relaxing on the couch or lying in bed, or could be watching with a group of friends. Again, taking immediate action isn't always likely.

I'm going to dive into direct mail in a little more detail for two reasons. One, there's more to talk about and two, I'm a huge fan. I realize there are many marketers out there who believe direct mail is old school, and not very effective in today's world. I have one word for them: Nope. It depends on what you're saying, who you're trying to reach, and what you're trying to get them to do. Direct mail is spectacularly effective in certain industries. Part of its beauty is that when people assume something is old school because of technology changes, they'll assume it won't work so they won't use it. Which means they've gotten out of your way, making everyone else's work better.

You need to consider your business, and what you're selling. If you're selling a $30 widget, direct mail most likely won't give you the return on investment you need. But if it's real estate or other big-ticket items or services, your ROI can be incredible.

Understanding this medium is fairly easy. First, direct mail is going to a mailbox, to a physical location. Second, if you acquire the right list, you can control the criteria and target the right type of person in the right location. If you need homeowners in a certain zip code, you can target them. Then there's the tactical, physical aspect of direct mail. Do you want to send a coupon or an invitation to a dinner seminar? Bingo!

As we've discussed with the other mediums, you also need to know your audience. Older people are more used to physical mail and younger people are more likely to just throw it away quickly, right? Actually, no. They both throw it away quickly so again, you have to make sure your message cuts through the clutter. Picture someone opening their mail while standing over a garbage can. "Trash, trash, bill, trash, trash, this looks interesting." It's just like picturing someone checking their email. "Delete, delete, delete, let me open this one."

While tracking the response matters for all mediums, it can be much more difficult in some than in others. If your direct mail piece contained a trackable phone number, you can see how many people called that number. You'll know, if you sent out X number of pieces, you got Y number of responses. If you double the number of pieces, and they go to an equally appropriate list, chances are you'll double the number of responses.

If you run a TV or radio ad with a trackable phone number, you'll know what kind of response it got. But many businesses make the mistake of using the same phone number across different mediums and different campaigns, making it impossible to determine which one had the highest response rate.

Billboards pose a different challenge. If you put up a new billboard for your pizza place and sales go up, that could be the reason. But you don't know that with certainty. People don't usually walk in and say "I saw your billboard and that's why I'm here" Whereas with banner ads, social media, email and other web-based marketing, usually all you have to do is count the clicks to gauge the response rate.

So an important part of understanding the medium is recognizing what you can track and what you can't.

Each medium has its strengths and weaknesses. Each can be extremely effective in specific situations targeting a specific audience. If you know what those are, and tailor your message accordingly, you'll be able to use each medium successfully, and get your conversation off to an effective start.

TAKEAWAYS FROM THIS CHAPTER

- Always be aware of the nuances of the specific medium you're using.
- Understand how your prospect is receiving your message through that medium.
- Be sure to carry the same message across all mediums throughout one conversation.

It's important to remember that your message is just words. How it reaches people and how they interact with it are very different on different mediums. Once you clearly understand the differences, this becomes automatic for you. You'll be able to tailor your message for that medium and that segment of your overall conversation, and keep the conversation going effectively.

CHAPTER 7

MISTAKE 2:
WRONG OR MISMATCHED OPENING TONE

When I say opening tone, I'm referring to the very beginning of a conversation with a prospective client. So it would be easy for you to conclude that means the first time you're talking to that person. But that's not the case at all. The medium doesn't matter.

Just because we're calling it a conversation, that doesn't mean you're actually talking. This is the first time you're communicating with a client. While it can be verbal, such as a cold call, it's far more likely to come in some type of marketing trigger piece. Maybe it's an email, or direct mail. It could be a billboard, or a radio or TV commercial, or an online ad. Whatever the medium, this is where your relationship begins.

Which means you have to be extremely careful about your tone. Because that tone needs to carry through every step of the conversation. If you start with the wrong tone, or change it along the way, you're putting yourself into a hole that will be difficult if not impossible to dig out of.

Let's say the opening tone is fear. That's common enough. Marketing that scares people into acting can be extremely effective. "Is your credit at risk? Are you protecting your family?" But you can't go from that opening tone to one that's warm and fuzzy. And if you think warm and fuzzy is the best way to close the deal, that's the way you need to open the conversation.

Remember, it's not the same person having the entire conversation. Marketing got it started, then sales picked it up. If a salesperson is talking to someone who replied to a "we're trying to scare you" ad, and the first part of that conversation is all sunshine and roses, the natural progression of a conversation isn't just broken, it's shattered. Rapport building? No chance. Now the prospective client may be thinking, "If it's really not that bad, why are you trying to scare us?" Now the salesperson has to repair something just to get back to even. You've created an issue.

When you pull a fire alarm, you get a lot of attention. But when it turns out to be a false alarm, you've created a lot of angry people.

One of the reasons this happens is, sometimes marketing is looking at the quantity of leads, not the quality. Maybe they've created 1,000 leads, but with the right tone they could have created 400 good leads and the conversations would have been better.

Think about a trade show. You're there trying to sell your product and show why you're better than others. It's costing you money and time. You want as many people as possible to come to your booth. So how many times have you seen a company hire a pretty model in short shorts and a tank top, and have her pass out fliers? That will certainly attract a bunch of people. But that's just activity, not productivity. Granted, if it's a tool show and it's all guys walking the floor, it could be helpful. But if it's a chiropractors' convention and the doctors are there with their wives and families, then it's not the best idea.

Activity vs. productivity. Quantity vs. quality. But you don't want to go too far in the other direction, because if you narrow your scope too far and only bring in a handful of leads, you may have a lot of salespeople just sitting around. There's a balance.

But it also depends on the value or profit margin of what you're selling. If you're selling helicopter engines, one sale a month might be outstanding. Their opening tone might be very, very specific, because it's narrowing down the field. They might know that if they talk to three people in the course of a month, and they're the right leads, they're going to close one, and it's a multi-multi- million dollar deal. Which comes back to knowing your client acquisition cost, and the lifetime value of a client.

But let's go back to the beginning. Now that you're focused again on beginning with the end in mind, let's talk about how you're actually going to begin the conversation. There are three key points to make. Your why, your what, and your how. In that order.

Here's why the "why" comes first. People don't care about the how or the what, until they know the why. Say you make cars. Big deal. Every other car company does that. How you do it doesn't matter….yet. You could have the latest, greatest, most amazing technology on the planet, but until they know the why, they still don't care.

"We make cars that will protect your family and make you safe and your vacations fun and take you off road." That's the why! And that's what people really care about.

Too often, people begin the conversation with, "This is what we do", and then they touch on the why. Tell me why you do it, and why I care. You have to do the why for both of us. Tell me why you do it, why I care, and why I should work with you. Then tell me what you do. Then, after that, if necessary, tell me how you do it. "We use the latest technology. We have the most highly-trained people." Think about how many times you've done this out of order, because that's the way you've been trained or that's just the way you thought would be the most effective.

The why sets your tone. And when you use the wrong why, you're starting off the wrong way. Earlier, I referenced fear, and the types of ads we see that use fear to get our attention. But when scary isn't the real why, you've put an alarm in front just to get more activity, and you've messed up the tone. Now you have to recover from that, and instead of continuing the conversation along its normal flow, it's now a conversation about why we scared you. "Sorry, we didn't mean to, we were just trying to get your attention." Now you have to get the conversation back on the right track, and get to the real why. At that point, you've probably lost some people. But many would say, "Why didn't you just say that in the first place?"

Always keep your why in mind. For example, I've worked with many people who sell solar panels. If their why is they love the earth, they want to protect the planet and be green, then that has to be their voice throughout the entire conversation. So if you want to do ads that talk about saving money, they still have to be in that voice. "You can save money while saving the planet." This is your voice and your tone. It's who you are. It's not your brand per se, it's your brand personality and your brand's mission.

If you're selling windows, the "what" is, "Hey, you can get new windows for your house," and the "how" might be, "Our windows are made better and are more energy efficient," but what matters to people is the "why". "Is your house drafty? Is it cold in the winter and warm in the summer? Are your heating and air conditioning bills too high?" The people you're talking to in this conversation already know they need new windows. They know they're going to buy them from someone. Why should it be you?

Nobody buys a drill because they need a drill. They buy a drill because they need a hole. The only reason you need new windows is because the ones you have are doing something wrong. They don't care about your double or triple panes, or your highly-trained crews. You may never talk about the how and still sell windows, if all they care about is the fact that their house is cold.

When somebody sells on the how or the what, they're basically saying, "We're open. We're in business. We exist." Those are the people who say their marketing failed, or direct mail doesn't work, or Facebook ads don't work, or seminars don't work. No, they do work. You're just doing them wrong. You're setting the wrong tone.

The message is more important than the medium. But you have to understand both. If you begin in the right order, and lead with the why, you're always going to be talking about benefits, not features. And benefits sell.

TAKEAWAYS FROM THIS CHAPTER

- The opening tone is where you first interact with a prospective client.
- It takes place on whatever medium you're using, so it can be verbal, written, or visual.
- This needs to carry through every step of the conversation.

However you begin a conversation with a prospective client, on whatever medium, be sure to begin with a tone that will continue throughout that conversation. Your "relationship" starts at this point. And of your three key points: what you do, how you do it, and why you do it, the why should come first. If you always begin with the end in mind, and keep the same tone throughout different stages of the conversation, through different mediums and different people, you'll keep the conversation on track and put yourself in the strongest position to close the deal.

CHAPTER 8

CASE STUDY: IN FOCUS

As we've seen, an important part of keeping the marketing-sales conversation going is making sure that your message and tone remain consistent throughout. That relates to your brand or image. Are you clear on that? Is it the right one for your product or service and the solution you offer? Just as important, is it what you want?

 Meet Bob Thompson. He's a photographer in Tampa who was one of my coaching clients. He was very successful, but he wasn't really doing what he wanted. Then the economy crashed and so did that version of his business, so it was an opportune time to re-invent himself. I helped him focus on the brand he really wanted, helped him market that business, and watched him take off.

His experience can provide valuable lessons for any business owner struggling with this challenge.

Scott: You're now a very successful commercial photographer. Let's talk about how you got to this point.

Bob: I had a pretty good run earlier in my career as a commercial photographer. I also did a lot of weddings, and a ton of high school portraits. But the economy tanked, I lost most of my high school contracts, and I closed my studio. I reverted to my commercial roots, and tried to make a go of it.

That's when you and I had a conversation that was pivotal for me. I still wanted to shoot all the cool, creative marketing and advertising stuff. But that had been steadily declining. You were pretty blunt with me. You said, "You're trying to specialize in too many things. You're trying to please everybody. From a sales and marketing standpoint, that doesn't do anything for you."

It wasn't easy to hear, because while I heard the truth in it, I didn't want to give up my attachment to what I considered the creative work I had spent my career doing. But as we went through this process, it became clear to me how the marketplace had changed in my business. Less and less money was being spent on marketing and advertising. Those are often the first budgets to go when money gets tight.

So we took a step back and asked, "What's something that's never going away? What's something that everybody is always going to need?" The answer to that was corporate headshots. So I began to really build my business around that particular activity. With a renewed focus, I've taken the ball and run with it. Now I'm knocking down headshots for 200 people at a time, and making more money in a day than I ever used to make doing the creative work that I thought I would miss so much. And I'm actually having fun doing it.

Scott: It wasn't easy to get you to embrace this change.

Bob: In our conversation, you challenged me to give up my attachment to that which I was afraid to let go of in my marketing efforts. But that generated a lightning rod for my business. Something I could use to pull business in, and then turn that business into the very kind of thing I wanted to be doing. Often I'll start out with headshots for a company, but they know my background and they'll see my portfolio, and next thing you know I get hired to do work well beyond headshots.

You had to help me get past how mundane headshots sounded to me. You got me out of my comfort zone. I had to get through the emotional baggage around what I was giving up. But your input was truly a pivot point for me. I switched mindsets and gave up that attachment to the creative ad photographer I was trying to maintain. Now I go boldly forth and say, "I do corporate portraits. I do head shots. And I do them well." I changed my business name, changed my branding, and haven't looked back since.

Scott: That's great, I love to hear that. Talk a little more about going through this process.

Bob: You just burned right through my reluctance and resistance. You saw where I was spinning my wheels, and made me see it. You have this ability to get to things quickly, get to the core of what's not right, and find a way to communicate it to get someone to scratch their head and say, "That sounds like a good idea. I should give that a try." Anyone who's having any kind of issues in their sales or marketing process would benefit from that.

Scott: In a way, this got you to think about things and say, "I wonder why I didn't think of that in the first place."

Bob: That's true. Retrospectively, that's exactly what happened. There was a lot of pride involved. I spent a lot of years building up to become this great commercial photographer with a very creative, impressive portfolio. Much like a long resume, you think staying with that path and building on it is always the best move. In this process, you coached me to get past the "image" that was in play around the kind of work that I was doing. As I said earlier, I'm making more money today, and having more fun. I am more focused on being the best at pulling the true best "you" out in every headshot. It's actually much more fulfilling than commercial product shots ever were.

Scott: How we ended up doing this is actually an interesting story. You never know how things are going to turn out.

Bob: Yes, I had originally hired you as a sales coach. And that led to us being friends for many years. But then we had that fateful, pivotal day. You made me understand that I needed something to be identified with in the marketplace. Something people would respond to, rather than me being the guy who said, "I can do anything. I can do this whole array of things." That gave people no avenue to see the key things in what I was offering. It led to the lightning rod concept that has served me so well, and let me build on what I had.

Scott: So now what? Where do you go from here? Are you where you want to be or is there more to come?

Bob: I want to keep growing. I'm now building a team of photographers that I'm training in the distinctions I possess and the type of work I do. I'm beginning to put them in place of myself in jobs I can't take, or using them in jobs that are better suited for a team. I'm actually beginning to build this company so it's not just me.

But it's still my brand. These photographers are part of Thompson Brand Images. That's who they represent when they're working for me. I'm not just hiring contracted guys to go out and knock stuff down for me. I'm giving my client base this team of crack-shot guys who are "Bob Thompson trained". They provide the same level of service and same caliber product.

I'm beginning to take this model and take it into the event industry, where I probably would be able to run a company like this. I can pay them fairly and still make a nice profit when I'm not there in person. That's a breakthrough for my company.

Scott: So you're not just Bob Thompson, photographer. You're Bob Thompson photography. Your team, under the Bob Thompson umbrella, with Bob Thompson's training and the Bob Thompson method. So growing your business this way has actually helped you set yourself up for retirement.

Bob: Yes, and it's the first time I've ever had a glimpse into that possibility for myself. I've been aware for a while that I could probably sell my business because I have a large client base and a good reputation in town, but that never looked too lucrative. Now that I'm starting to diversify and spread it out a little more, it does begin to look like something I could build.

Retirement is an interesting word. I've never really looked at that, because I'm physically fit and let's face it, photography isn't like digging ditches or doing roof work in the Florida heat. I'm taking photographs, most of the time in beautiful places, of successful people.

But looking ahead and seeing the potential to get enough wheels under this so it can keep rolling if I want to bow out and let the guys take over, is an awfully exciting prospect.

TAKEAWAYS FROM THIS CHAPTER

- If you try to specialize in too many things, it does nothing for you from a marketing standpoint. You can't please everybody.
- Sometimes you need to get out of your comfort zone and lose your emotional baggage, and take your business where it needs to go, not where you want to be.

Working with clients like Bob has helped reinforce the value of truly understanding your brand, and how it relates to growing your business. If your approach is too broad, and you're trying to be all things to all people, you'll fail to reach any of them effectively. Often, a company is reluctant to let go of certain products or services, or fails to see the marketability of others.

MISTAKE 3:
USING JARGON

Jargon:

1. The language, especially the vocabulary, peculiar to a particular trade, profession, or group: *medical jargon*
2. Unintelligible or meaningless talk or writing; gibberish
3. Any talk or writing that one does not understand

I think the dictionary's definition of jargon makes it clear. It's not something you want to use. (Did you notice the word "gibberish" in #2?) Who wants to be accused of using gibberish?

Let me add a fourth definition: Language used to make someone look smart, but which in reality comes across as, "I'm better than you," and annoys the hell out of the person who reads it.

But if jargon is so bad, why is it used every day in every type of marketing? I think that's where my fourth definition comes into play. I believe people get caught up on getting specific on certain things. There's nothing wrong with that. It's good to be specific or detailed. It helps increase your credibility and sell the "how" of what you do. But there are people who want to show how smart they are. How experienced they are. And they use jargon to make the point. "I've been in this industry for 20 years, and I know all the codes, and I have a PLR-17 with the JPT-654 and I'm certified as a J-27." Say what?

Your customers may not have a clue what you're talking about. And even if you think they do, you're only going to get the C-personalities. You're only going to get the people who are detail oriented. Now if you sell to engineers, and you sell something very "engineery", and that very specific thing is the unique selling proposition, then it's okay to touch on it. But remember in real-life communicating, nobody talks like that. We're in a world of texts, of shortcuts, and BRBs and LOLs and so on. There's a mechanism in the text that is acceptable because that's how people are trying to get a quick message to you, get you information, and then keep moving.

Whether people are speaking or writing, they often have a tendency to try to prove to you how smart they are. Remember, people don't care how much you know until they know how much you care. Which is why we always want the "why" first. What are we working on and why do I care? If my communication to you is, "I understand you, and I understand why this matters to you, that's why we come up with a solution," then jargon would have nothing to do with that.

When I say industry jargon, we're often talking about codes, or specific words, or anything that's a shortcut in your business. Nobody would ever order a hamburger and ask the waitress, "Can I get that medium rare with no setups?" Everyone in the restaurant world knows the setups are the lettuce & tomato & onion, etc., but no one says that. That's not how we communicate.

But people like to use terms they know in their world. I had a collection agency for a client, and they had little acronyms for literally everything they do, because there are so many legal requirements and so much agency regulation. So they're always saying things like, "They have a DEF on their CR because they BPR," or "Approved by the CFPB," or a whole bunch of other initials. But does everyone know that the CFPB is the Consumer Financial Protection Bureau? Too many times people abbreviate when they need to say or write the whole thing.

Using industry jargon isn't just used as a description of your product. Sometimes it's used to shorten things, like the headline in a banner ad. Which actually is a worse offense, because now there's no context around it. There's just an ad that people see.

There are certainly examples of industry jargon that have made it into the mainstream. But that still doesn't make it right to use them. Case in point, SEO. Anyone who has a website knows that means search engine optimization and it's important. But it's not how you begin the conversation. Instead of starting with, "Are you good at SEO?" you can ask people, "Are the people who need your services finding your website?" Now you're leading with the why in a way that relates to people.

So even if 90% of the people you're talking to probably know your industry jargon, you still should avoid it, or at the least, limit how you use those acronyms or specific industry terms. Are you totally, 100% certain everyone you're sending this to will know it and understand it? If you have any doubt, leave it out.

I'm not saying dumb it down to a fifth grade level, where your marketing piece looks so dumb it makes you look like you don't know what you're talking about. Let's go back to SEO. If you're using that as a scenario, maybe you're trying to get a message across that even though there are 80 million views on the internet every hour, that doesn't mean you're going to get any of them. Just because something is available, doesn't mean it's going to be seen. If my house is for sale, and it's on the internet, everyone in America can see it. But that doesn't mean I'm going to get 300 million views. I may get a couple dozen, but the real number that matters is the number of people who actually came to look at my house. All the SEO jargon in the world isn't going to change that.

Let me make it clear, I'm not saying completely eliminate industry jargon. I'm saying control it or limit it, and only use it when appropriate. Certainly avoid it when trying to get your initial message out. But once you've engaged with somebody, and you're further along the conversation, you have a chance to understand how much they know about what you do. That's when you may be able to start inserting some of your jargon. If you're talking to the webmaster of an online retail outlet, of course he's going to know SEO and SRM and CRM and all the initials you use, so use them to your heart's content.

In addition to limiting your industry or brand jargon, also be careful about using your products' names. They don't necessarily contribute to the conversation. When I worked at BIC, every pen had its own name because they sell them retail in other ways. So we could say, "If you're looking for retractable pens, or stick pens, we have those categories and can help you with lots of them." But when it got specific, where there was only one pen in that category, and the name made it clear, then you could say "four-color pen". In most cases though, it was far more important to say, "executive style" than the product name, which was *Citation*. So even if you aren't using industry jargon, you may have gotten too crafty with the brand name. *Featherlite* makes sense, if it's the lightest one you sell. But if your product is named *The Patriot*, how does that help sell it? When the name makes sense, use it.

Part of the battle over jargon relates to the conflict between sales and marketing. A marketing person knows, "Don't say certain things. Let it marinate a little and then come out." Salespeople have a tendency to say, "Sell them. Get them all the features and the benefits right up front." As we've discussed earlier, it's better to pique their interest early so you can get them to move toward you. Remember, the foundation of your communication is going to be natural progression. Get somebody interested, get them to inquire or let you connect with them, then win them over in that process, and then take their order.

There are reasons to leave things out at the beginning. It's like you're taking baby steps. First, I want to make sure you're interested in things like what we do. Kind of. Then if you are, you'll probably want to look into it, because they're not all the same, and ours is different. Then if you look up the differences between ours and others, you might find that we do this, and you might want to know how we do it. So after leading with the why, now we're getting to the what and the how.

It's always important to keep your goals to a single step every step of the way. The goal of the email or letter is to get you to say you're interested. You contact me, or I'll contact you. The next step is the appointment, where you listen to them. Part of listening to them is understanding what issue/problem they have. Or maybe they're confused about possible solutions. Now you can present your solution to them, and most likely shorten their sales cycle.

But with industry jargon, if you go too early, you may lose them before they raise their hand. However, once they raise their hand and say, "That interests me, because I have an issue like that where a solution would help me," now you're listening to them, and you may realize, "Okay, they do understand more." You can start hitting them with the details of that. Industry jargon is better suited when you're talking about the how. If you haven't done the why or the what, you can't get into the how, and you can't get into your jargon.

Speak to express, not to impress

I understand how important credibility is. But using jargon isn't going to make you more credible if you can't back it up. This happens a lot of times with new entrepreneurs. Someone who's been in an industry for a long time and now breaks out to start their own company. Usually their first few marketing pieces are downright horrible for this reason. They want to make sure everyone trusts them. "Look, I know I have all the answers. I may be a brand new company, but I've been in the business for 20 years. I need to make sure people who are concerned because we're new, trust me and know I'm experienced." So they hit people with jargon, and all they've done is confuse people.

What you'll find is people usually don't care how long you've been in business as long as you're focused on a solution that helps them with an issue. There's that "why" again. The mature marketer, whether they've been in business for one day or 40 years, knows, "I always have to focus on what's in it for them, and what I'm asking them to do." So whatever the delivery method is, you're going to send a piece of information that has to be crystal clear about two things: There is or may be an issue, and we have a solution to that issue if it fits you. Then if you want to know more, this is exactly what I want you to do. If you can't fulfill that criteria on every marketing piece, you're going to have disconnects.

It's going to be hard to judge the mechanism in which you delivered it, because you failed the message. Even if it's just a banner ad. "Do you have this issue? Click here." Here's the issue, and we can fix it. Is it a long-form letter? Okay, go into more detail. Use testimonials. But don't give it all away. An effective long-form letter doesn't lay out the entire process and tell you how to fix it. It says, "Here's an issue. Here's an example of somebody having this issue. I told you it was an issue. Here's another example of this issue. Here's how this person solved it. Here's a person who had an issue and we solved it and this is them thanking us. If you want more, call this number."

When the prospect says, "I have this issue and I'm currently looking for someone to help me with it,", or "I have a solution I don't think is working, so I'm exploring other options. Can you give me some detail of the difference between what you do and what I currently use?" this is your opportunity to get into details. You can use some of the how.

But if you're going to use industry or brand jargon, or acronyms or things like that, it needs to be in a place where you're almost 100% certain they already know what you're talking about before you say it. Because what happens is people try to use it as to impress, and this is where you'll get fast-talking, shiny, slippery salespeople. Someone who tried to over-talk. Who tried to dazzle with B.S. This is when your prospect decides they don't like you. And if they don't like you, no matter how smart you try to prove you are, they also won't trust you, and then they don't care to know you, which means they'll never buy from you.

The goal of your relationship with any customer is to win them over based on a solution that helps them, not you. If you focus on industry jargon, or brand jargon, most of the time you're really just talking about yourself.

TAKEAWAYS FROM THIS CHAPTER

- Make sure you limit your use of jargon, and only use it when appropriate.
- You want to increase your credibility, but not do it in a way that talks down to people or confuses them.
- Your goal should be to convey a solution that meets their needs.

A good rule of thumb is to avoid initials, acronyms, and phrases that are a shortcut in your business. Successful marketing and salespeople know that using industry jargon too much, or too soon in the conversation, will lose people, not impress them or make them more motivated. Make your message solution-oriented and you'll win them over.

CHAPTER 10

MISTAKE 4:
THE CHALLENGE-TO-SOLUTION GAP

Here we are at the midpoint of the seven mistakes. We're also at a key point in our conversation. This is where that brick wall becomes something you can't step over. This is where the continual conversation can separate and veer off. The challenge to solution gap is where the natural progression of a conversation can break down.

This often becomes a natural separation between the marketing and sales teams. The marketing team is saying, "Hey, we have to get more creative to get more leads." This is where somebody may be pushing a salesperson to answer specific questions which he can't answer, because the conversation has veered off. If marketing starts to pull away toward their own goal, they can create this issue. When everything works, your tone sets the stage and everything follows accordingly. You run into a problem when something takes the continuum of a conversation on a sharp left turn or makes it hit the brakes. Now it gets tough to continue effectively.

No one needs to write a book to tell you, "Don't say your product does something it doesn't do." You don't need to buy a book for that. You should know that. Your integrity can stand for itself.

However, what many people don't realize is if the conversation between sales and marketing isn't so smooth, or if each has very specific goals that differ from the other's and can separate, this is the point where that can happen. From a marketing perspective, it could be, "To generate more leads, I can make a feature or benefit or challenge seem bigger than it really is." This is where statistics often come in. "89 percent of people are scared of this," but none of the people calling in seem scared. But maybe that's because the fear factor was the wrong approach.

Your salespeople will detach from the topic if it's too far out. You often hear a salesperson say, "Once the calls come in, I'll just do my own thing." Now they're the ones who have created the gap in the conversation.

To overcome that, whichever side is causing it, this middle point of the conversation could be an ideal time to retouch on salespeople and marketing people working together. You want to always be thinking of the continuity of the conversation. It's okay to have some differences, but they can't be dramatically different, or certainly not oppose each other. I believe what happens is if either side is only focusing on what they care about, they have a tendency to break the conversations and confuse the clients.

That confusion isn't always clear. That prospect on the phone isn't going to say, "Okay, I'm confused. I'm not sure why I'm here." But what you'll notice is your funnel will begin to get a flat spot right there. You'll have a lot of calls, but things aren't converting. The calls seem to be getting harder. Salespeople say, "I feel like I'm spending more time at the beginning of a call recouping a conversation than I am continuing one." It's that awkward turn, and you're feeling it.

The callers, who at this point are not turning into customers, aren't turning away because they're angry. They're indifferent. And that's worse. Anger isn't the enemy, indifference is. It's becoming very difficult if not impossible to keep the conversation going forward, because you now have this giant obstacle in front of you. It's this giant wall of indifference. It's this giant wall of "I don't care about what you have to say anymore."

This is where marketing people have a tendency to add a little spice to the recipe to try to get more leads, and salespeople end up with indigestion.

Salespeople will get exhausted with having to start conversations all over again. It's no longer a sales call where you feel like you're talking to a prospect and moving them through the process. Instead, you feel like you're starting at zero. Or less than zero. You have to dig yourself out of a hole and come back up. You're working harder than you should, and you aren't getting the results you want.

If there's both a sales manager and a marketing manager involved, this is the time for them to huddle up and get things back on track. If not, as it starts to separate more and more, if it keeps going and no one is paying attention, all of a sudden after a month or two you discover sales are slipping and you're nowhere near where you should be. Depending on what you sell, this could be a very noticeable and very costly problem in a moderately short period of time.

Let's say your product or service has six key benefits, and you know that two of them are what makes you really different. So you keep focusing on them. However, customers may not really care about the ones that make you different. Instead, they may care about one of the other benefits, which everyone else also does. So now the challenge becomes focusing on that benefit, but doing it in a way that still makes you different.

There are financial advisors who say they have the best investment product available. Then a client comes in and says, "Oh, I've heard of that. Everyone has that." It's like a checking account. You can get one at any bank. So in reality, you're not selling a product, you're selling yourself; your service, your attention to detail, the things that make you stand out. People can get the product anywhere. But if they can't get the help they really need elsewhere, the actual solution that makes you different, now the conversation becomes much smoother.

Often, when I talk about the challenge to solution gap, it's not the issue or the problem that's the challenge.

For example, the problem could be you're in pain. Severe, debilitating pain that's keeping you from living your life the way you want. Then you see an ad, or get a piece of direct mail, and the message is, "Are you tired of living through pain?" That's a very effective message, if what they're trying to sell you actually stops pain, especially your type of pain. In this case, they're talking about stem cell therapy. And if stem cells don't work on your type of pain, they've started that conversation in a way that's going to make it very difficult to convert you into a customer.

You have to know that your product or service can deliver on what you're promising. If stem cells work on certain types of pain, promote the heck out of that. But don't say, "Whatever your pain, this is your solution." Because now when someone comes in with the one type of pain it really doesn't help, you've created a challenge to solution gap and you have to overcome it.

It's not, "Are you in pain?" It's, "Is your back pain keeping you from picking up your grandchildren?" It may be shoulder pain or knee pain or joint pain, but it may not be migraines. Part of what creates the challenge to solution gap, is when the challenge is too broad. You may have three or four or five different challenges, with a broad umbrella covering all of them. All those challenges need to funnel down to the one solution you're offering them in this portion of the conversation.

However, if the solution doesn't match or is confusing, you have a problem. Here's an example, staying with stem cells. (I'm not picking on stem cells, it's just a good example and I have experience with this.) I've done a lot of work with a stem cell provider. At one time, they bounced around the idea of this marketing message: "Are you tired of crazy medical bills?" Here's the logic behind that. If you're suffering from knee pain long enough, you're going to see your doctor frequently, you're going to take a lot of pain medicine, and eventually you'll probably need a knee replacement. All that adds up to a ton of money. But if you received stem cell therapy and it worked for you, you don't need the surgery. It will save you a lot of costly medical bills.

But here's the gap between the challenge and the solution. Stem cell therapy costs money. And it's an out-of-pocket expense, not covered by insurance. If someone comes in saying, "Yes, I'm sick of my medical bills," and they learn they have to pay for their stem cell therapy, you've made it much tougher to keep that conversation going. It's more difficult to close the deal. When you create the challenge yourself, you've created the gap. Yes, there's still a connection there, but the gap may be too big.

This comes back to the "why". The challenge should always be their why. "Are you in pain? Do you want to save money on your electric bill? Do you want to save the planet?" You want to target the why that will get them to do the thing you want them to do, which is continue the conversation and hopefully become a customer.

But if you've created a gap between why they need you and what you do, you get the reaction every salesperson dreads. "Well, let me think about it." Which really means "No thanks."

You've created indifference. Which, as I talked about earlier, is the opposite of "I like it" when it comes to sales. Not "I hate it", just "I don't care." And which may be tougher to overcome than dislike, because there's no emotion there. And the worst part of that is you're the one who took it away.

TAKEAWAYS FROM THIS CHAPTER

- Always be aware that the solution needs to match the challenge, otherwise it will cause the conversation to break down.
- Often this is where there's a breakdown between marketing and sales, but if you make sure both teams are on the same path, you'll keep the conversation on track.
- The challenge should always be their "why".

It's all too easy to create this gap, whether it's in an effort to create more leads, or an attempt to close deals with prospects who are expecting a different solution than what you're offering. But when sales and marketing teams are unified, and remain focused on why the prospect needs your product or service, the solution will match the challenge, the conversation will remain unified, and you'll have the best chance of closing the deal.

CHAPTER 11

MISTAKE 5:
A ONE TRICK PONY:
MANUFACTURED
URGENCY/FOCUSING ON LOGIC
OR EMOTION ALONE

While I'm calling this mistake a one trick pony, we're actually looking at two elements here. Manufacturing urgency, which we know is a huge mistake because it gets them in the door but doesn't get them to buy, and then focusing either on logic or emotion by itself.

If you're a single topic seller or marketer, essentially what you've done is make it easier for yourself, but you've limited your audience. There are different personality types, different buying styles, and different buying cycles. People act in different ways. There are different ways to motivate them. You've taken an audience that could be broad if you were better at communicating with everyone, and limited it just to people who would only respond in a certain, specific way.

Granted, you've made it easy because you can duplicate all your materials. It's certainly easier to train salespeople. You just turn them loose. "Use this and we'll get more." And if the volume plays out, some people are happy with that, but that may not be the most potential for your business.

Emotion can be a very effective sales tool, but only if it's done properly. Let's say you only work on fear, or you only work on a scare tactic, or your sales method is pressure for the sake of pressure. That's not an effective use of emotion, like trying to get through to people because you really care about them. In that case, there are layers of emotions.

But you're sticking to one single emotion. Fear can be multiple things. You can have awareness. "Hey, watch out for...." People who sell insurance virtually always have an element of fear. "Is your family protected? What if something happens and you're not covered?" The fear is always lurking there, but the layers of emotions come with, "You'll be able to sleep better. You'll have peace of mind. You're protecting your family."

People listen in different ways, they gather information in different ways, and they make purchasing decisions in different ways. When you are a one trick pony you will lose the others that you potentially could have gotten. That may be by choice, but I think potential is more valuable.

Which segues into manufactured urgency. "You have to do this today or you're going to miss out." Then... "Okay, we'll give you one more day." People are smart enough to see through that. There was a time, years ago, when people did one-day sales and it really was just one day and you could get a pretty good deal on something. But when you do a one-day sale twice a month, every month, it's not special and the deals aren't special. It's part of your rhythm. People get your emails and learn your patterns and those surprise sales aren't much of a surprise.

I see people get caught up in their business and look for ways to make it easier for them to have a sale. It's easier to schedule and it's easier to promote. And there are times logistically it does make sense. But I always say when you make it easier for you, you inadvertently make it harder for your audience. If you're going to have a monthly sale, call it a monthly sale and let people know about it.

This may sound like I'm slamming retailers, but I'm not. There are specific instances to use this in retail. If you're Walmart or Target or someone with multiple product lines, and you are looking to increase the number of visits based on separate topics, it's a great strategy. Someone comes in to buy electronics, and then you send them something about cookware or another category. You want and need them to come back. But that's not manufactured urgency. In this case, they're intentionally trying to get someone to come to another department. Think of it as crossing the lease line. Every time somebody steps across your lease line you have a chance to sell them another item.

That's different than a company that has a limited scope of products, or is trying to get more clients based on their single topic to a single audience.

Sometimes the manufactured urgency is based on commissions. Sales teams may want to get more sales before the end of the month. Or you're trying to close out your books for the quarter. That's "your" need. So how do you make it beneficial and believable to the customers? You create an added value benefit for them to act sooner. If there's something in it for you, make sure there's something in it for them. "If you buy a car this week, we're throwing in three extra oil changes and 10 more car washes."

I've also seen businesses change their calendar month when they see their audience has caught on. Their business month might go from the 15th to the 15th. Their month-end sale is actually in the middle of the month. The salespeople get their commissions and the customers don't see it that way.

You may like the one trick pony because it's easier for your account. Or it makes it easier to calculate commissions. Or because that's how your rebate cycle comes from your manufacturer. Or it makes the numbers look good in your quarterly report. But if what you're doing is self-serving only, you're going to have issues with it no matter how much urgency you convey in your marketing. If it doesn't help them, they're going to sniff it out. It's going to be predictable. Even worse, it's disingenuous, and eventually you're going to lose business.

You're actually hurting your audience in several ways. One is you're limiting them because you're not going to attract all of them with this approach. Second, if you do it too much it's obvious and they'll sniff it out. And third, your integrity. Your story or your brand is a lie. How good do you think that will be for your business?

So let's flip the switch from emotion to logic. Bearing in mind, a lot of people will say all sales involve emotion. Whenever there's a sale, it was an emotional decision. And yes, there's emotion involved in your decisions in whatever you do.

But we're focusing on how you try to sell your product or service. In this case, it's one or the other. Logic or emotion. Either one limits the scope of people who respond that way.

I know what you're thinking. "I sell to engineers. I sell to computer programmers. I need to sell on logic." Of course you need to talk to your audience in a way they understand. If that's engineers, they require facts and they require accurate information. Certain professions and personality types require data to make their decision. But there will be no sale, even with the most C-type personality or the most logically-thinking engineer, if there's no emotional reason to do it. You're not selling to Mr. Spock (and even he had some emotion). No matter how logical the purchase is, buyers still want to feel good about the decision. Whether that's bragging to others about how awesome their software is, or how they were able to increase profits and efficiency, there's still emotion.

We've all heard the saying, "facts tell, stories sell." If all you do is list fact after fact after fact, and then tell people to call 1-800 whatever, they aren't going to call. You have to put facts in the stories, but you have to make it clear why the facts matter. If you're just selling by spec sheets, or data, or the formula, without giving people a reason to care, they won't care and they won't buy.

This may sound very computer and engineer focused, but think about this: "Better ingredients. Better pizza." Does the commercial go on about how the ingredients are made, how they're shipped, the farmers and chemists involved? No, the rest of the commercial is about how it tastes and how you can have parties with pizza. They told you some facts, and sold you on emotion.

As I mentioned earlier in this book, I work with some companies that sell windows. They might sell the most technologically advanced window on the planet, with the same materials NASA uses on the space shuttle, but once a logic-centric person looks at all that information, what makes him actually buy the windows? Not because it was six times tempered. Because he can sit in his recliner in front of a window on the coldest winter day and not have to cover up with three blankets or have an arctic breeze blowing on him. And having the same technology in your house as the space shuttle is kind of cool.

When you're reaching different personality types and different information delivery types, and you have logic and emotion built in, with the emotion being clearer because of the facts, this is where that continuum starts to be real smooth. This is where your audience might widen a little bit.

You may ultimately sell a few people specific to what your product solves. But in the marketing-sales conversation from beginning to end, when we say open the door, this is opening the door wider. You want your door all the way open so more kinds of people can come in.

But keep this in mind. We're at mistake number five. If you've made some of the first four mistakes, or you haven't done the first steps in the continuum properly, you may have compounded your issues to the point where you get almost no response.

Not knowing what kind of door to open, not opening it all the way, using the wrong words at the door, are all things we need to be aware of and need to avoid.

Here's something else that complicates the conversation. You may need to reach different types of people in one conversation. You may have an engineer check out your product, and someone else be the decision maker. The detail-oriented person may be the gatekeeper. So you have to get them to say, "This is valid enough to work with. Let's explore further." But as you reinforce the facts with them, you have to make sure you're still reminding them of the "why". No matter how many facts you're delivering, you have to keep the "why" in there.

One last point for this chapter. The one trick pony can travel across every type of medium we're using. Humans learn different ways. Visual, auditory, kinesthetic, and so on. Whatever medium you're using at this point in the conversation, keep the one trick pony out.

You may be using long form direct mail, with copy only. No graphics, no pictures. That can be very effective in certain industries. But that's a lot of content. And if it's nothing but facts, it's not going to work. Plus, at some point, you're going to lose some of those visual people. They'll read most of it, but then need to see a diagram of how it works or some other element to keep them engaged. Or you need to bring that up in another stage of the conversation.

Again, when I say conversation, it's the continuum from the very first trigger piece to the closing of the deal. Throughout the conversation, there needs to be visual and audio, text and images, data and emotion.

Because just like there are multiple buying decision types, there are multiple information gathering types, and different learning types. That last one is a big one. Some people learn by hearing, some people learn by seeing, and some people learn by doing.

So any of those times you can engage people multiple ways, you'll get more people engaged, which can only be better for you.

TAKEAWAYS FROM THIS CHAPTER

- Manufactured urgency will get someone in the door, but it doesn't get them to buy.
- Focusing on either logic or emotion ALONE limits your audience and how you can engage them.
- This is especially important because you may be reaching different people throughout one conversation.

Your prospects are smart enough to know when you've manufactured the urgency. Doing that could delay the sale, or lose the prospect entirely. Focusing on logic or emotion alone could work in limited situations, but there are many different personality types and buying styles, and you may want to reach several of them in one conversation. Using both logic and emotion strengthens your position, and the facts can actually make the emotion clearer.

CHAPTER 12

MISTAKE 6:
VERBALS AND NON-VERBALS DON'T MATCH

Let me begin by saying I know there's a lot of information out there about this subject. If you're in sales or marketing, chances are you've read at least one of the many books dealing with this. You may have even had the "Law and Order" concept drummed into you. You know, the one about detectives watching you more than listening to your answers when they interrogate you, so they can "see" if you're lying.

Take a deep breath. I'm not taking it that far. My goal for this chapter is to help you understand how this fits in the continuum of the conversation, from marketing's introduction to sales closing the deal. So let me start by clearing the air a bit.

Chances are, everything you've read contains these numbers, which everyone from salespeople to psychiatrists know to be true. Your communication breaks down this way: Seven percent your words, 38 percent your tone, and 55 percent body language.

So when you're face to face with someone, like an in-person meeting or a conversation at a trade show, you have to control all three. If you're on the phone, you lose the body language element, so you have to get the most out of the remaining 45 percent. If someone is going to know, like and trust you over the phone, you have to work a little harder.

Also consider there are times the conversation is not from one human to another. It may be the point where we've sent an email or a piece of mail, so it's words only, right? No tone, no body language. So you're trying to communicate with only seven percent of what you can actually get through to somebody in our verbal/non-verbal world. But your brand and your image can be the non-verbals. The look of the message, its quality, and how consistently your brand is conveyed. In other words, how you come across to someone.

So, this chapter will look at all of that.

Let's begin with this example. You're on the phone and talking about something that's urgent, but you're talking slowly and you're acting indifferent. "Yeah, the sale ends today. If you want to do it, that's cool." That sounds ridiculous, doesn't it? But let's say you tout the technological innovation of your company, and your website loads slowly and the video won't start. This is the part where many people say, "Oh, I get it."

So for the sake of this conversation, non-verbals can be everything your prospect can actually see about you that's not what you're telling them. The e-commerce company whose website is difficult to navigate. Or something that once again sounds ridiculous, but I've actually seen. A company that stresses family values, but uses scantily-clad models to drive traffic to its booth at trade shows. Things like this break the flow of the conversation, because sales or marketing didn't pay attention to their own image.

Here's a saying I live by, and preach constantly to my clients: **You can't read your own label from the inside of your bottle.**

It's very difficult for someone to say, "This what it looks like for somebody who's talking to me." Do you ever record your sales or marketing calls and listen to them afterward? Do you seek feedback from others on your team?

Let's bring in the company that may be the best in the world at this. Disney. I always tell people, "Go stand in your own line." Disney makes their ride engineers and people who manage traffic flow through their parks stand in those lines day in and day out. They want to know, "Okay, you're a third of the way through? Are you getting impatient? Is there anything for you to look at? How can we get you to stay?"

When there's a long line in the drive-through at Chick-fil-A or In-N-Out Burger, employees walk to the cars further back in line and take their orders. That's not just to be helpful. You're less likely to give up and leave if you've already placed your order. If you haven't ordered and you get frustrated, you can leave. If you've ordered, your tolerance actually quadruples.

Smart companies that sell at trade shows send someone up to a salesperson and pretend they're a customer, to see what it looks like from there. How are they dressed? What does the booth say? Does it make someone feel like they'd want to do business with you?

Let's go back to that website. If your site says your company is family-owned and gives its customers personal attention, the user is more likely to stick around if it's a little slower to load. There's your non-verbal. But if someone does stick around, and when they get to inside pages of the site the words change and no longer match the brand, or an image is offensive or never loads, your non-verbal has become a problem.

This matters no matter where you are in the continuum of the conversation, and no matter what the medium.

Here are a couple other examples you've probably seen. A company's message is, "This sale is a big deal, we never have sales," and you go to their website and see the last 10 sales. Or, "This is a limited-time offer," and they make the same offer the next week. Or one of my favorites. "Top quality. The highest integrity." Then their site tells you to join their discount club and get 80 percent off. Outlandish discounts are difficult to accept. Literally unbelievable. There must be something wrong with it. It's a disruption in your "know, like, and trust." Because I can get to know you, and I can get to like you, but I'll never trust you.

Let's go back to the example where you only get the seven percent because you can only control the words of the message. Guess who's adding the tone? The reader. So you have to be very careful with the words you're going to use. As my grandmother used to say, you can't keep someone from adding their spice to your chili.

Here's a piece of advice that's not just relevant to this. It also covers many aspects of our lives. "You can only control the things you can control." You can plan your dinner seminar months in advance and invite the right people and have a great presentation, but if there's a blizzard or tornado or flood or power outage, you're out of luck.

If I'm having a face-to-face meeting with a prospect, and I do a good job of controlling all three facets and the entire 100 percent, I have the highest likelihood of winning you over, gaining your trust, and having you believe what I'm saying. Once you veer from face-to-face, you start to lose more and more. However, as I mentioned earlier, there are other things that take the place of body language and tone. The look of your email or letter is your "body language". If it's filled with typos and misspellings, and doesn't look professional, they're thinking you don't have your act together. This is something we're actually hard-wired to believe. It's not something a sales guru made up. Psychiatrists and psychologists will tell you, it's how our brain is wired.

If it's a phone conversation, the prospect's brain is painting a picture of you. They might never have met you or seen what you look like. You can't control how your voice makes them picture you. People might picture me as six foot two with a full head of dark hair. If you've seen my picture on the book's cover, you know the hair part isn't accurate. But you can control your tone.

Now let's take that one step further. Phone conversations aren't always just over the phone, and face-to-face conversations are not always face-to-face. People do sales meetings via Skype or Zoom or FaceTime. Maybe one person is doing a webinar and 30 people are watching. So the setting is the nonverbal. If you're in your office, how does it look? Are you doing it from home? Are you in your car? You can set the tone for a conversation like this, but the setting, or what's going on behind you, has to match what you're saying.

You have limited body language. You do have your expressions, and the way you tilt your head and lean in. Those are all real. But what's going on behind you can take over. If you're doing Skype or Zoom or FaceTime, don't for a second think they're focusing only on you. They're looking at the picture on the wall behind you, or your cat in the background, and if it is distracting, they're no longer listening to your words.

Let's look again at the entire marketing-to-sales continuum. From the beginning of the relationship to the end, the verbals and non-verbals need to match. Say it begins with a TV commercial. Maybe that's how you met your AC guy. What you saw in that commercial, what you heard in conversations, and what you experienced when he came to your house have to be consistent. Nothing can disrupt the flow, or interrupt the know, like, and trust.

Did he pull up to your house in a truck like the one you saw on TV? If the commercial talked about protecting your carpets, did he put something over his shoes? Those are non-verbals. Those add up to, "Trust me. I'm not going to just show you something on a commercial and then not do it when I get there." If you're going to show it and say, "This is how we do it," then have that be the way you do it. Amazon has a very consistent image message: We're going to get it to you. You're going to get a box at your front door. It's going to have a smile on it.

In the continuum of the conversation, marketing sets the tone and sales carries it through. And here's the key part. You don't have to take a leap with a non-verbal to get to the sale. It's more important that you do nothing non-verbally to hurt your sale. Because by the time you're having that conversation, they have interest. You don't want to do something to disrupt the progress.

There's a tricky thing people like to try to do. We've all heard someone say, "Listen, I'm not really a salesperson. I just educate. I share information. I just want people to make an informed decision." Right. And they have a bridge to sell you. Everybody knows that every business is in business to make money. It's the car dealer saying, "We're selling you this car under invoice. We're going to lose money on this deal." Nobody believes that.

This also carries through the delivery of the product or service. I talked about the AC guy putting covers on his shoes to protect your carpets. If you're a window company, and part of your image is that you leave people's homes better than you found them, but the guys who do the installation at my house track mud in from outside or gouge a wall, or they smell and leave their smoky odor behind, the verbal and non-verbal stopped matching at a critical juncture.

I hate to say this, but I've had clients who are financial advisors who were doing seminars, and I literally had to tell them, "Remember to brush your hair. Wear a tie. Iron your shirt." Sometimes what happens is people are so wrapped up on delivering their words of their sale, they lose track of the other aspects. If I'm your client, and you're asking me to trust you with my life savings, shouldn't you have your act together and look professional?

But when the non-verbals portray "I run a respectable business. Yes, I charge for it, but you're going to be very happy with the results just like all my other customers," you're sending the message you want and need to send.

That's what I mean by what I said earlier about not being able to read your own label from inside your bottle. If you're so wrapped up in "your" message, or you're so convinced that "My business is my baby. This is my dream and what I want to do," then "your" words may come across as self-serving and run the risk of coming across as not credible or not believable or not trustable. It's surely okay to have passion for your business, however, your audience may feel like you are focused on pleasing your interests over theirs.

If the verbals and non-verbals of your conversation don't match, and the three aspects of your communication don't add up right, you've made it difficult if not impossible to make the sale.

TAKEAWAYS FROM THIS CHAPTER

- Communication consists of 55% body language, 38% your tone, and only 7% your words.
- Looking at how your prospects or clients are seeing you and receiving your message will help you make sure all three aspects are in sync.
- If you're not in a position where all three are in play, make sure you do control the ones that are.

An effective marketing-sales conversation matches the verbals and non-verbals throughout, which reinforces prospects' ability to know, like and trust you. Always look at yourself and your message through your prospects' eyes. When you're in a face-to-face setting, be aware of the three components of your communication. When you're on the phone, or in another setting where you lose a component, make sure you control the ones that remain.

CHAPTER 13

MISTAKE 7:
MISSING OR INCOMPLETE WRAP-UP AND CLOSE

Congratulations! You've made it to the finish line. You're at the final stage of the marketing-sales conversation. All you need to do now is close the deal.

Again, we're talking about the conversation from the beginning, whether that was a marketing trigger piece or a verbal "Hi my name is," or however it began, all the way through every stage, to this point. Because everything you've done up till now had only one goal in mind: to get to this point and make the sale.

But this is where a lot of salespeople get what we call "happy ears". Someone sounds like they're about to say yes. So you get them to say yes. And your work is done, right? Not so fast. Often that doesn't really solidify the sale, or make it cancel proof. So let's look at how to avoid that, and make sure that when you think you've closed the deal, you really did close it.

Incomplete wrap-up refers to people slipping into "take the order mode," even though their product really requires more.

If you've done it right throughout the conversation (and chances are you have, because the prospect has made it to this point) you've remained focused on meeting their challenges. A big part of closing the deal is going through those things. Because if the client believes what you have will fix their need, they're going to say yes to whoever they get at this point. But if in reality that specific need won't be met by your product or service, even if you're going to solve all their other issues and this really is a good product for them, they're not going to be happy. It doesn't do the one thing they wanted. And because the salesperson had happy ears, he heard the yes but didn't pay attention to the why. So you've come all this way, and in the end you've broken the chain.

Sometimes people sell right past the close. By jumping to the YES, they skipped a step. So it's incomplete because they didn't verify what was specifically needed. A vague or general solution is sometimes okay, but can also "not" be a solution in the long run. If they would have taken just a little longer, they might have found out that another version of their product or service would have done it just fine. Everything would have been great, and they still would have gotten the sale.

The wrap-up is not just what you say to get the yes. It's also some of what comes after the yes, and how the customer feels after they've said yes.

I certainly don't need to remind you to make sure your product actually does what you say your product does. But I think many people assume the other person gets what it does do, when sometimes they don't. So I always recommend that in your close, there should always be a questioning conversational aspect. Let them come to the determination.

I find the best salespeople, who are most consistent on a regular basis, put themselves in a position to get the client to decide to buy from them. They don't push. Hard closing really only works in very few industries. Pushing hard and being aggressive, "sign here now," only works in so many places.

The decision making process has changed significantly over the years. When my parents or grandparents were told by a doctor or police officer to do something, they did it. No questions asked. Now, everyone questions everyone all the time, and they want to make the decision for themselves.

Consider this: people have access to options, literally in the palm of their hand, even while they're sitting right in front of you. They may sit right there in your office and pull out their phone and Google your competition with you watching.

Which is why I say, in your wrap-up, you should always bring them back to the beginning. So always ask questions. "When you received our letter, I remember you said this. What were you thinking then?" Keep doing circular recap. "Now that I've learned a little more about you..." Doing this reminds them why they're here in the first place.

Also, even though they've made it to this point, their enthusiasm could have cooled off along the way. That competitor they Googled in front of you may have made a very competitive proposal. A lot of things can change between your intro and today. So recapping and getting them to remember things can be helpful.

It's always good to clarify what prompted them to look or respond in the first place. And then, as you walk them through, "When we met you said this. Then we discussed this. You brought up this. I proposed this." It's also a good way to clear up any misconceptions. A proper wrap-up can lead them to say, "Yes, that's why I'm here. Yes, we did talk about that. Yes, I remember changing course." And most important, "Yes, this is what I want." So if they leave and still have any kind of misunderstanding, or shift gears in their head, you've done your part to make things as clear as possible. You've made your wrap-up as complete as possible.

You know I like analogies. Here's one that fits this subject. You're looking forward to the weekend. You and your wife are going to go out to dinner, to a place you've been talking about for a while and heard great things about. Your relationship with this restaurant started the first time you heard about it, or the first time someone referred it to you. The relationship continued to grow as you checked out their website and saw the menu and what the place looked like. Then you called to make a reservation, and the person on the phone treated you great. So you arrive, and it's a beautiful restaurant. You place your order. And the waitress disappears. You wait and wait and wait for your meal. Even your bread and water.

That's the incomplete wrap-up we're talking about. That's the feeling people can get when they work with any company. "I placed my order. You got my sale. And now when I need one more thing, I'm getting nothing from you." That's a real feeling people get from retailers, whether they're brick and mortar or online. People get that feeling from service providers, such as insurance companies or financial advisers. That feeling of, "You got my money and I never heard from you again." Or, "When you wanted me to buy, you always returned my call right away, and now you never call me back."

You've just broken your own relationship.

Mature and successful salespeople understand this. Because once you've gone through a long cycle of selling, or you understand your product and your customer, you truly understand their need. You understand that they have a challenge and you can solve it. The good ones don't have happy ears. They listen to what's really being said.

The last thing you want is to have it really easy before the yes and then absolutely agonizing afterward. So I always say, customers are just going to do what customers do. You are trained at what you do and it's your job to do it right. You are shepherding them through this process.

It's like the Dog Whisperer. If you watch him on TV, you know, he doesn't really train dogs. He trains people. Dogs are going to do what dogs are going to do. No, I'm not calling your customers dogs. I'm saying people are just going to do and decide and think and discover and make decisions how they do it. It's our job to help coach them through the process of decision making, understanding your solution to their need, and making sure they match. So they feel good about the purchase. They look forward to its arrival. They're excited that it's going to work. And then when it works, they feel good about it and tell others about you.

Often, a rookie or unseasoned salesperson just hears the yes and thinks, "Who cares? I'm getting my commission." But then there may be 15 more calls with the client, and the sales manager is yelling because things weren't clarified and the customer didn't get what they expected. When you're on the phone with an upset customer, you're not able to be on the phone with a new customer. So it becomes very counter-productive.

Which is why I say, do the work upfront. Take them through the natural progression, and don't push too hard one way or another. They may be moving faster and faster downhill, and saying "Yes, I want it. Get it here as soon as possible." You can and should still say, "Okay, I just want to make sure I'm sending you the right thing. You sound like you need this accomplished soon. So the last thing I want to do is send you the wrong thing." Then you can pull them back, and be sure the sale doesn't just close, it closes and sticks. Remember, everything up till now has been focused on getting you to this point. It's worth it to finish these last couple steps to make sure they're clear about what they're buying, they're happy with what they're buying, and they see the value.

Now if you've reached this point and they say, "No, I don't think so. Not yet, anyway. Let me sleep on it," that doesn't mean it's the end of the conversation. But it usually is an alarm that says you didn't share the value with them, or you missed their need, or you solved something that wasn't their primary need. Somehow you've missed the mark. Or, they truly have a root need that you can't solve. Using a questioning wrap-up, you can see where you veered off the path of their need's analysis, and you can clarify the solution that they actually do need.

Throughout these chapters, we've talked a lot about the tone and the message, and how they have to sync up and remain consistent throughout this conversation. It's especially critical at this point. Because this is the why. Why they're here. Why they want this. And when you're at the end of the conversation, the why has to be front and center.

If you did anything to break the conversation or disrupt the flow along the way, you're going to pay for it here. This is where you're going to get caught. This is where the salesperson might have to answer for marketing tricks. "Your ad made it look like the sale is only today, but now you're telling me I have till tomorrow." They might have been hurrying because they thought they were going to miss out on something, but now they might be angry enough that you may lose them entirely.

And remember, if you do close the deal, it's not the end of the conversation. It's the end of the prospect relationship and the beginning of the client relationship, which are both part of this one fluid conversation. So if the wrap-up wasn't right, the client relationship could be off to a bad start, and it could end fairly quickly.

But for now, let's wrap up the 7 mistakes. Throughout, you may have noticed, everything we say and do should almost always be focused on them. If you know and understand your prospects, what their needs are and how they operate, as long as your product or service truly meets their need, you have a pretty good shot at keeping the conversation alive and ultimately closing the deal in a way that makes it stick.

What's their need? Is this something they'd like and would make their life a little more convenient, or is it a "hair-on-fire" need? Two completely different tones. Understand them. Speak to them in the appropriate tone. Clearly understand their issue or need. Make sure you can actually solve it. And then make sure that when you're talking to them, you have the same tone. You've always talked to them the same way. You clearly understand who they are. You have other clients like them and you do this all the time. If you keep working through this list, you'll see how smooth it can be.

Of course that doesn't mean you're going to sell 100 percent of the time to 100 percent of the people. But if you get in front of people who truly have the need that your product or service can actually solve, and you take every possible step with them, you've given yourself your best chance of success.

Then the other things just happen as they happen. Sometimes, a prospect wants your product and needs it, but just can't afford it right now (or get approved for credit). You can't control that. You can't control what you can't control.

But look at all the things we can control. How we speak, how we listen, what we say and how we say it. You have to shine all of those at the highest percent of likelihood. In the end, you're going to get some yeses and you're going to get some nos. But you'll get the most yeses you could that were available to you. And you can't ask for more than that.

TAKEAWAYS FROM THIS CHAPTER

- Good salespeople know there's more to the close than getting your prospect to say yes.
- Your wrap-up should always bring them back to the beginning, and reinforce what got them interested in the first place.
- This is the point in the conversation where it's especially critical that the tone and message are in sync, and the "why" is front and center.

Smart salespeople know there's much more to closing the deal than getting them to say "yes". You need to solidify the sale. If your close is incomplete, you might take the order, but if you haven't reinforced how your solution meets their challenge, the prospect could believe you're meeting a specific need, which might not be accurate. Ultimately, you may get a cancellation to that same sale. It's important to bring them full circle, back to the beginning of the conversation. It all comes back to the "why".

CHAPTER 14

CLOSING THOUGHTS:
CLOSING THE DEAL

Now that we're approaching the end of this conversation, which began 116 pages ago, here's what I hope you got out of it and where I hope it will take you.

Your takeaways will be different depending on whether you're in sales or marketing, but my goal is that no matter which side you're on, you see the connection between the two, and how critical and beneficial it is to have a unified message.

Most people think of sales and marketing as two different things. And while they are different in task, they're almost never different in goal. If you separate the two, and think of the goal for marketing as more leads and the goal for sales as close more sales, you create the divide we spoke of earlier.

But if you can look at sales and marketing as one big piece, a starter and finisher that always have to happen and always have to be in harmony, you're focused on the big picture. Think of a restaurant. When you get a bad meal, the restaurant failed you. If your server brought you the wrong order, the cook could have prepared a perfect meal and it's still a fail. Those two people have to work together in unison to have a happy customer, or they run the risk of losing that customer.

One of the bigger takeaways I hope you think about, especially on the sales side, is words. A lot of salespeople spend a lot of time on the words they say once they're in front of the customer. Which is a good thing. But you really should understand what marketing said to get you in front of the customer, and then expand on what the prospect really cares about.

I'm not saying don't have the attitude that if you get in front of a warm body you'll do fine. Every good salesperson has that confidence. Even cockiness is a good thing at times. But if both sales and marketing look at the big picture and expand their view of their responsibilities, from sales over to marketing and from marketing over to sales, you will by nature become better and better and better as a team.

If a quarterback throws the ball to the right spot but the receiver isn't there, or the receiver is in the right spot but the pass wasn't, either way it's an incomplete pass. Or worse, an interception. Teammates depend on each other. So do sales and marketing. They have to get it right in order to get clients. If you haven't figured out by now, I'm a huge proponent of client acquisition. I think everything you do in your business should be laser-focused on acquiring customers.

Then you can focus on customer service. And getting referrals. Because one very important benefit to having a unified marketing-sales conversation is sales can deliver what marketing talked about, which is what the client wants and needs. And when you deliver what a client wants, you have a happy customer, and happy customers are going to refer other customers.

But that's not going to be your primary source of new customers, so it still comes down to client acquisition. At the end of the day, if you have the continuum from marketing through sales to closing the deal, and you get better and better at it, you've created a process that works. You can plug more people into that process and get more clients. You can keep it going.

Client acquisition will never be an issue for you. The normal threats to a business, such as client attrition or one-time buyers never giving you repeat business, will never scare you if you're really good at acquiring new customers.

Often, salespeople get wrapped up in the finish line, not the race. They get so focused on the finish line, it's easy for them to be separated from where the client might still be at the starting gate. But they might have to back up to meet them and bring them to the finish line.

Expanding your "responsibility view" gets you focused on the whole race. That doesn't mean salespeople are going to work in marketing, and create print pieces and direct mail. But if that salesperson goes to a trade show, what marketing did in terms of messaging and words and signage are all on display at their booth. So what salespeople say to prospective clients has to match what's right in front of them.

As I said about direct mail, your relationship starts at the mailbox, and you want to keep it from ending up in the garbage can.

This is what I do with my clients every day. This is what I've done with hundreds of companies, from start-ups and small businesses to those on the Fortune 500. Because no matter what size your company, there are things you can do to improve your client acquisition. Think about it. If you could move your needle just five percent on a $20 million company, what's that worth? If you're starting out or trying to grow, and you could knock one thing off your learning curve, what's that worth?

Because what we do works. It works really well. But you have to do it, and you have to do it the way we tell you to do it. Let me tell you about a client that didn't do that. We laid out their path. We gave them 15 steps, and told them exactly what to do in each step. Well, they didn't like a couple of the steps, so they just left them out. They got in front of over 90 prospects, only got three appointments and didn't close any of them.

They called us back and said, "We remember you told us we could hire you to do this for us, and speak to our prospects for us." We do that, because it's an effective way to educate our clients. But we charge a lot of money for it, because we're now their sales force. I said, "Just to be clear, you're going to pay us a lot of money to do the things we told you to do, and when you watch me, you're going to see that all I did was what I already told you to do." They said okay, and we closed over 15 new clients for them that week. The good news is, they now do it the way we showed them and they're closing the deals.

So now what? What do you do with what you've gotten from this book? You have two options. One is to use what you learned, and make sure your sales and marketing teams are on the same page and you have the unified conversation that opens the door and closes the deal. It would make me pleased if you do that. I wrote this book to be that type of guide.

But you may want more than that. You may want to learn more, both about the process and about yourself. This book may have answered many of your questions but led to new ones you hadn't thought of. You may want to ask me those questions.

Maybe you can. Because you got this book, and made it all the way to the end, you may be eligible for a special opportunity. 30 minutes with me. I call it my "deal maker or deal breaker" consultation. It's the one I've had with people from businesses ranging from start-ups to Fortune 500 firms. In just that half hour, we can look at your challenges and see what solutions are possible.

But one piece of advice. Don't expect coddling. If I think you're doing something wrong, I'm going to tell you, and I won't be subtle about it. The good news is, it's fixable.

Obviously I can't do this for everyone who has this book. Only for those who qualify. To see if you do, go to www.socialdynamicselling.com/consult and fill out the questionnaire.

If you qualify, you get the half hour for free. And that could be the end of our conversation. Or it could go further.

I work with people on a short-term, medium-term or long-term basis. From a one-time consultation to a 30-60 day plan, to an ongoing relationship that could mean monthly or quarterly meetings or has ended up with me serving on company's boards. It's all solution based, and it's all about acquiring clients.

Because that's what it's all about for me. Helping people build their business and acquire more clients. You make more money. Your family eats better. Your employees' families eat better. I've come a long way since I was that kid "manipulating" his babysitter or parents. I've learned a lot about sales and marketing, about opening more doors and closing more deals. It's helped me do better than I ever thought possible. But the more people I share it with, the more people will also do better, and that's the biggest payoff.

So let's have that conversation.

To see if you qualify for a "deal maker or deal breaker" consultation, go to:
www.socialdynamicselling.com/consult

WANT TO
PUBLISH A BOOK
LIKE THIS?

BMD PUBLISHING HAS PUBLISHED DOZENS OF BOOKS
LIKE THIS IN NUMEROUS BUSINESS SECTORS.

OUR PROCESS IS EFFICIENT AND EFFECTIVE.

IF YOU'VE ALWAYS WANTED TO DO A BOOK BUT
DIDN'T KNOW WHERE TO BEGIN, GO TO
WWW.MARKETDOMINATIONLLC.COM/BMDPUBLISHING
TO SET UP A FREE *TURN THE PAGE* CONSULTATION.

BEGIN AN EXCITING NEW CHAPTER IN YOUR LIFE!

IT'S YOUR TIME TO BECOME
AN AUTHOR

Made in the USA
Middletown, DE
15 February 2021